THE WAY
TO RESPONSIBLE
GOVERNMENT

THE WAY
TO RESPONSIBLE
GOVERNMENT

The Constitutional Re-Structuring America Needs

Patrick J. McGrath

Writer's Showcase
presented by *Writer's Digest*
San Jose New York Lincoln Shanghai

The Way to Responsible Government
The Constitutional Re-Structuring America Needs

Writer's Showcase
presented by *Writer's Digest*
an imprint of iUniverse.com, Inc.

For information address:
iUniverse.com, Inc.
620 North 48th Street
Suite 201
Lincoln, NE 68504-3467
www.iuniverse.com

ISBN: 0-595-12508-5

Printed in the United States of America

Table of Contents

CHAPTER I

Why Change Is Needed

"The Constitution is not honored by blind worship. The more open-eyed we become, as a nation, to its defects, and the prompter we grow in applying with the unhesitating courage of conviction all thoroughly-tested or well-constructed expedients necessary to make self-government among us a straightforward thing of simple method, unstinted power, and clear responsibility, the nearer we will we approach to the sound sense and practical genius of the great and honorable statesmen of 1787. And the first step toward emancipation from the timidity and false pride which have led us to seek to thrive despite the defects of our national system rather than to seem to deny its perfection is a fearless criticism of that system."

WOODROW WILSON, *Congressional Government,*
1884 (page 215)

Note: Quotations and page references to Wilson's "Congressional Government" (hereinafter "CG") are taken from the 1956 Meridian/World Publishing Co. edition, with an introduction by Walter Lippman, reprinted by Peter Smith, Gloucester, Mass., 1973.

I am a patriotic American. I want the best for my country. I believe the time has come for Americans to realize, as Woodrow Wilson understood over 100 years ago, that the constitutional structure under which we live is almost the worst possible imaginable.

Americans live with the best constitutional principles possible—the rule of law, popular sovereignty, limited government, and the self-evident truths about the God-given rights of human beings. I propose to demonstrate that the structure erected to execute those principles—based on the concepts of "separation of powers" and "checks and balances"—have led inexorably to the chaos, confusion, contempt, and choler directed by the people against their institutions of government.

A better way is not only possible, but also workable. Under this system, many nations, free and democratic—most of whom share a culture of language and laws with us—govern themselves in a way that allows full debate of contentious issues, disposes of governors who do not hold the confidence of the people, and is, for the most part, free of the corruption and money-obsessed politics in which we now find ourselves.

I have included in the Appendix drafts of a constitutional structure that would fulfill these needs. There is a draft Federal Constitution and a draft State Constitution based on Responsible Government and the principles outlined in this book.

I have endeavored to anchor these drafts in the constitutional principles we hold dear, while at the same time putting responsibility at the heart of government.

Responsibility is a singular. Division of responsibility results in no responsibility. Do not these two words describe the political landscape in America today? Do not these two words provide the reason why it must be replaced?

Woodrow Wilson came to the same conclusion and condensed the problem into eight words: "no leaders, no principles; no principles, no parties." (CG, p. 11) That Wilson's insights hold up after more than a century supports the wisdom of his analysis.

Here I am compelled to explain to you, the reader, how I came to these conclusions. I believe the best way to do this is to present a short sketch of a political autobiography.

CHAPTER II

A Sketch of A Political Autobiography

A. Child at the Fall of Giants

"The informing function of Congress should be preferred even to its legislative function. The argument is not only that discussed and interrogated administration is the only pure and efficient administration, but, more than that, that the only really self-governing people is that people which discusses and interrogates its administration."

Congressional Government, page 198

I was born in 1960. Which means that my answer to the question, "What were you doing when John F. Kennedy was shot?" would be, "Probably playing with my favorite orange Tonka Toy dump truck."

That would have occurred in my parents' apartment in upper Manhattan. Two years later, my family moved to a townhouse in West Haverstraw, in northern Rockland County, New York.

West Haverstraw was a backwater, but I was content. Mark Rudd's rioting at Columbia University was only 35 miles away. It was on another planet as far as I was concerned.

I do remember where I was when Spiro Agnew resigned, October 10, 1973. I was in the eighth grade of St. Gregory Barbarigo elementary school in nearby Garnerville. I regularly read the newspapers and watched Walter Cronkite, so I was aware of national events, but Miss D'Alessio's solemn announcement to our class at the end of the day left me quietly stunned.

Ten months later, on August 9, 1974, I had cake and ice cream, not because Richard Nixon had resigned but because it was my sister's birthday. Three weeks later, I entered North Rockland High School, a singularly graceless block of a building that was then only six years old. Between entering there after Nixon's fall and putting on the tasseled cap four years later came a significant period which requires a separate treatment.

B. Eyes Opened in the Long White Cloud

I had my period of adolescent rebelliousness, not against my parents, but against my peers. My Catholic school was a home, but public high school was madness, and I wanted out. An out came.

In the beginning of my sophomore year, word came through that the local Rotary Club was participating in Rotary International's long-established program of high school student exchanges. I applied with alacrity.

My first choice was to go to West Germany, because I was studying German at the time. I was told that slots for Europe were already assigned, but there were plenty of openings for Australia and New Zealand.

After the interview process, I was accepted to spend the 1976–1977 school year in New Zealand. The Rotarians of

Waitara, a farming and meat-processing town in the Taranaki district on the west coast of the North Island, had agreed to host me.

I was picked up in Auckland by one of the Waitara Rotarians, the principal of the borough's middle school. My host and his wife then brought me to their hotel, but not before he had to stop at the annual national convention of middle school principals, which was why he was in Auckland.

After a 16-hour flight, I was in a total daze as he led me around the halls of the Commercial Travelers' Club, but my funk disappeared when he introduced me to a distinguished-looking gentleman. I asked who he was. That was Sir Keith Holyoke, the former Prime Minister, I was told. So here I was, hours off the plane, barely conscious, shaking hands with one of the best-known political figures in the country.

Sir Keith was by this time, of course, out of the loop. Everyone knew who was the real authority in the country—Prime Minister Robert Muldoon. Described by the country's leading comedian as a "well-known gross national product," Muldoon, when tarred by an opposition Member of Parliament with the nickname "Piggy," riposted by pasting a poster of a pig on a wall of his summer cottage.

Muldoon had taken office the year before when he led his National (conservative) Party to a trouncing over the now-opposition Labour Party. The Labour leader he had routed said Muldoon's victory felt like "being hit by a bus."

Though Muldoon didn't know it, a remark he made in a newspaper interview stuck in my mind. I didn't realize its significance at the time—otherwise I would probably have kept the clip. But I recall that Muldoon said that he would much rather be Prime Minister of his country than President of the United States because he had much greater authority than a U.S. President. "Now why would Rob make that kind of remark?" I asked myself. When I returned to America the truth of Muldoon's words was demonstrated.

C. The Belly of the Thompson's Gazelle

When I was halfway around the world my country decided to replace Gerald Ford with Jimmy Carter. I came back to find a new grin on the walls of the post offices.

From my point of view, the central event of the Carter Presidency was not the Iran hostage crisis but the second Energy Crisis of 1979. The Georgian declared that solving the Energy Crisis was "the moral equivalent of war."

Along with the rest of the country, I thought that the crisis was good as solved. The President sent up to Capitol Hill a package of five bills that would "solve" the problem. This will be a snap, I thought. The President is a Democrat; both Houses are controlled by Democrats; the President has declared it "the moral equivalent of war"; pas de probleme, n'est pas?

Non, une grande probleme, ami. The five bills were ripped to shreds, and everyone had a little knife in the ripping. It was incredibly enlightening some time later to see a PBS documentary special about the event, and see the political hurricane at work. No—hurricane is the wrong simile; it was like watching a natural history documentary, seeing the hyenas ripping open the belly of the Thompson's gazelle on the floor of the Serengeti Valley.

Right in my face, Rob Muldoon's analysis proved correct. From that moment, I was a convinced parliamentarian. The Georgian was sent back to his peanut shed a year later.

Across the "pond," in 1979, the British had decisively rejected the Labour politics of discontent and returned power to the Conservatives led by a woman of force, Margaret Thatcher. A year later, we replied by electing a man of resolve, Ronald Reagan.

The difference between the two was that Margaret Thatcher, because she had a working majority, solid principles, and a definite plan, could get things accomplished, while Ronald Reagan was constantly hamstrung. Why? Because Thatcher and her Conservatives controlled the whole political process in her country, while an American President, any President, controls no more than half the process, and if the Supreme Court is in a bad mood, the President controls even less.

Consider this question. Would the Iran-contra crisis of 1986 have been necessary at all if Congress had not shackled the Administration with restrictive legislation—the Boland Amendment—against support for the Nicaraguan anti-Communists?

In a parliamentary government, George Schultz and Caspar Weinberger would have presented their policy openly to the House, telling them that the U.S. would support the contras with whatever was needed, and defended that policy openly. End-around plays and clandestine trips would have been unnecessary.

D. The Cattle Show in Iowa

In 1987, I moved to Ames, Iowa, as I was awarded a graduate assistantship in the Journalism and Mass Communication Department of Iowa State University (now the Greenlee School of Journalism and Communications). In addition to research—my M.S. thesis was on "The International Knowledge of Beginning Journalism Students"—I took the opportunity to practice some high-level journalism that came right into my backyard.

1988 was the year Americans would choose a successor to Ronald Reagan. The path began in Iowa, with its now legendary precinct caucuses in February. That year's caucuses were the first since 1980 where both Elephants and Donkeys would be on the campaign trail.

In October 1987, the Republican Party of Iowa rented out the Hilton Coliseum in Ames, the home of the Iowa State Cyclone basketball team, and held what it called a "Cavalcade of Stars." I decided to cover it for the radio station back in Rockland for which I had been a "stringer."

For an admission fee of $25, Iowa Republicans could hear stump speeches by George Bush, Bob Dole, Jack Kemp, Alexander Haig, Pete du Pont, some minor-leaguers, and the surprise of the season, Rev. Pat Robertson. When Robertson walked up to the podium, all the cynical heads of the press corps in the peanut gallery twisted their necks. The Robertson supporters were going bananas. They had even brought a pep band. Not surprisingly, Robertson won the straw poll taken at the event—because he had, in effect, stuffed the ballot box by bringing out more bodies to Ames than the others.

What I remember most happened when I was out playing journalist, sticking my microphone under delegates' noses. I would ask, "Why do you support Bush—Dole—Kemp—Haig—Robertson— du Pont—whomever?" Since most delegates were wearing someone's buttons this did not need a preliminary question.

Again and again, I received answers that started with the phrase, "The man I send to Washington…"—as if the respondent, and only he, would be allowed to choose the next leader of the Free World.

In other words, the delegates saw themselves not as Republicans or Democrats but as partisans of a person. I had seen this in other contexts, but never so directly. I had seen thousands of sheets of campaign literature that said, in effect, "Vote for me, and I will to X, Y, and Z, and I will save this state/city/county absolutely single-handedly!" Only rarely did I see literature that said, "Vote for me, I'm a Republican/Democrat because that's what I believe in."

In effect, there aren't two parties in Congress; there are 535 parties, one for each Representative and Senator. The amazing thing is that anything gets accomplished at all. Five years later, the weakness of this system was demonstrated again.

E. Return of the Hyenas

Bush was in, Bush was out, and in 1993, for the first time since 1980, both ends of Pennsylvania Avenue were in the hands of one party.

The Arkansan, filling the role of the Georgian, declared that solving the "crisis" in health care would be the Great Accomplishment of his administration. Once again, the country thought that passage would be a "done deal," with a Democratic White House, Democratic Senate and Democratic House of Representatives. What was "done" was another meal of Thompson's gazelle for the hyenas of the Hill.

Woodrow Wilson analyzed and understood the problems of the Clinton attempt at health care reform more than 100 years before the legislation was introduced:

> "The voter, moreover, feels that his want of confidence in Congress is justified by what he hears of the powers of corrupt lobbyists to turn legislation to their own uses. He hears of enormous subsidies begged and obtained; of pensions procured on commission by professional pension solicitors; of appropriations made in the interest of dishonest contractors; and he is not altogether unwarranted in the conclusion that these are evils inherent in the very nature of Congress, for there can be no doubt that the power of the lobbyist consists in great part, if not altogether, in the facility offered him by the Committee system." (CG, page 132)

It is in this spirit that I propose an American version of a system that has the capability to short-circuit these nightmares.

CHAPTER III

The Critique of Pure Madness (Your Guide—Professor Wilson)

"Our long national nightmare is over."

> —*President Gerald Ford, speaking to the nation after the resignation of Richard Nixon, August 1974.*

"The American people are now and for some time have been asking to be allowed a good night's sleep. They're asking for an end to this nightmare. It is a legitimate request."

> —*Former U.S. Senator Dale Bumpers (D-Arkansas), defending President William Jefferson Clinton during his impeachment trial, January 1999*

Are recurring nightmares a sign of health in the body politic, or a sign of disease?

> —*Patrick McGrath*

Woodrow Wilson published his *Congressional Government* in 1884. He had a Victorian writer's love of the run-on sentence; otherwise it would be worthwhile to reprint the whole of his small volume here.

Instead, I will present here selected extracts from his book, to demonstrate that the constitutional problems of 1884 are the same constitutional problems of today.

Wilson's fundamental criticism was that, in the end, because of "separation of powers," no one is fully responsible for anything in our government.

> "If there be one principle clearer than another, it is this: that in any business, whether of government or of mere merchandising, *somebody must be trusted*, in order that when things go wrong it may be quite plain who should be punished....*Power and strict accountability for its use* are the essential constituents of good government. A sense of highest responsibility, a dignifying and elevating sense of being trusted, together with a consciousness of being in an official station so conspicuous that no faithful discharge of duty can go unacknowledged and unrewarded, and no breach of trust undiscovered and unpunished,—these are the influences, the only influences, which foster practical, energetic and trustworthy statesmanship. The best rulers are always those to whom great power is intrusted in such a manner as to make them feel that they will surely be abundantly honored and recompensed for a just and patriotic use of it, and to make them known that nothing can shield them from full retribution for every abuse of it. It is, therefore, manifestly a radical

defect in our federal system that it parcels out power and confuses responsibility as it does."

(CG, pages 186–187; emphasis in original)

Wilson forthrightly cast the blame for this directly on the hallowed statesmen of the Constitutional Convention, and secondarily on those who worshipped the Convention's "work product" as if it were the unalterable gift of demigods:

"The main purpose of the Convention of 1787 seems to have been to accomplish this grievous mistake. The 'literary theory' of checks and balances is simply a consistent account of what our constitution-makers tried to do; and those checks and balances have proved themselves mischievous just to the extent to which they have succeeded in establishing themselves as realities. It is quite safe to say that were it possible to call together again the members of that wonderful Convention to view the work of their hands in the light of the century that has tested it, they would be the first to admit that the only fruit of dividing power had been to make it irresponsible."

(CG, page 187)

Wilson realized what Gilbert and Sullivan wrote in *The Gondoliers*: "When everyone is somebody, then no one's anybody." Or as Wilson put it:

"This, plainly put, is the practical result of the piecing of authority, the cutting of it into small bits, which is contrived in our constitutional system. Each branch of government is fitted out with a small section of responsibility, whose limited opportunities afford it to the conscience of each many easy escapes. Every suspected culprit may shift the responsibility upon his fellows. Is Congress rated for corrupt or imperfect or foolish legislation? It may urge that it has to follow hastily its Committees or do nothing at all but talk; how can it help it if a stupid Committee leads it unawares into unjust or fatuous enterprises? The Secretaries aver that the whole mischief might have been avoided if they had only been allowed to suggest the proper measures; and the men who framed the existing measures in their turn avow their despair of good government so long as they must intrust all their plans to the bungling incompetence of men who are appointed by and responsible to somebody else. How is the schoolmaster, the nation, to know which boy needs the whipping?"

(CG, pages 185–186)

Wilson foresaw that this division could lead to a crisis in an emergency:

"Congress must act through the President and his Cabinet; the President and his Cabinet must wait upon the will of Congress. There is no one supreme, ultimate head—whether magistrate or representative body—which can decide at once and with exclusive authority what shall be done at those times when some decision there must be, and that immediately. Of course this lack is of a sort to be felt at all times, in seasons of tranquil rounds of business as well as at moments of sharp crisis; but in times of sudden exigency it might prove fatal—fatal either in breaking down the system or in failing to meet the emergency. Policy cannot be either prompt or straightforward when it must serve many masters. It must either equivocate, or hesitate, or fail altogether. It may set out with clear purpose from Congress, but get waylaid or maimed by the Executive."

(CG, page 186)

Furthermore, the members of the Cabinet are only partially responsible to Congress. Those conservatives who loathe Janet Reno's Attorney-Generalship could see her testy relations with Congress foreshadowed by Wilson one hundred years earlier:

"Congress stands almost helplessly outside of the departments. Even the special, irksome, ungracious investigations which it from time to time institutes in its spasmodic endeavors to dispel or confirm suspicions of malfeasance or of wanton corruption do not afford it more than a glimpse of the inside of a small province of federal administration. Hostile or designing officials can always hold it at arm's length by dexterous evasions and concealments. It can violently disturb, but it cannot often fathom, the waters of the sea in which the bigger fish of the civil service swim and feed. Its dragnet stirs without cleansing the bottom. Unless it have at the head of the departments capable, fearless men, altogether in its confidence and entirely in sympathy with its designs, it is clearly helpless to do more than affright those officials whose consciences are their accusers.

"And it is easy to see how the commands as well as the questions of Congress may be evaded, if not directly disobeyed, by the executive agents. Its Committees may command, but they cannot superintend the execution of their commands. The Secretaries, though not free enough to have any independent policy of their own, are free enough to be very poor, because very unmanageable, servants. Once installed, their hold upon their offices does not depend on the will of Congress. If they please the President, and keep upon living terms with their colleagues, they need not seriously regard the displeasure of the Houses, unless, indeed, by actual crime, they rashly put themselves in the way of its judicial wrath."

(CG, pages 179–180)

The way around this, Wilson believed, was to have "the representative body [i.e., Congress] to have all the executive servants of its will under its close and constant supervision, and to hold them to a strict accountability: in other words, to have the privilege of dismissing them whenever their service becomes unsatisfactory." (CG, page 181)

"Inquisitiveness is never so forward, enterprising, and irrepressible as in a popular assembly which is given leave to ask questions and is afforded ready and abundant means of getting its questions answered.

"There is some scandal and discomfort, but infinite advantage, in having every affair of administration subjected to the test of constant examination on the part of the assembly which represents the nation. The chief use of such inquisition is, not the direction of those affairs in a way with which the country will be satisfied (though that itself is of course all-important), but the enlightenment of the people, which is always its sure consequence. Very few men are unequal to a danger which they see and understand; all men quail before a threatening which is dark and unintelligible, and suspect what is done behind a screen. If people could have, through Congress, daily knowledge of all the more important transactions of the government offices, an insight into all that now seems withheld and private, their confidence in the executive, now so often shaken, would, I think, be very soon established. Because dishonesty can lurk under the privacies now vouchsafed our administrative agents, much that is upright and pure suffers unjust suspicion."

(CG, page 196)

Wilson also saw that in the vacuum of accountability, the Press could ask questions, where Congress could not or would not. Wilson had in mind the Horace Greeleys, James Gordon Bennetts, and Joseph Pulitzers of his day, but understood that the Press had limitations:

"…the utterances of the Press have greater weight and are accorded greater credit, though the Press speaks entirely without authority, than the utterances of Congress, though Congress possesses all authority. The gossip of the street is listened to rather than the words of the law-makers. The editor directs public opinion, the congressman obeys it." (CG, page 207)

"One of our chief constitutional difficulties is that, in opportunities for informing and guiding public opinion, the freedom of the Press is greater than the freedom of Congress. It is as if the newspapers, instead of the board of directors, were the sources of information for the stockholders of a corporation. We look into correspondents' letters instead of into the Congressional Record to find out what is a-doing and a-planning in the departments. Congress is altogether excluded from the arrangement by which the Press declares what the executive is, and conventions of the national parties decide what the executive shall be. Editors are self-constituted our guides, and caucus delegates our government directors." (CG, page 200)

In our own day, reformers have attempted to attack the problems of our constitutional system by "end-around" plays. These reformers have not even considered attacking separation of powers, because of their devotion to the "literary theory" of constitutional power. One such popular "solution" is term limits; Wilson was able to dissect this fallacy nearly a century before it became a household word:

"Administration is something that men must learn, not something to skill in which they are born. Americans take to business of all kinds more naturally than other nation ever did, and the executive duties of government constitute just an exalted kind of business; but even Americans are not Presidents in their cradles. One cannot have too much preparatory training and experience who is to fill so high a magistracy. It is difficult to perceive, therefore, upon what safe ground of reason are built the opinions of those persons who regard short terms of service as sacredly and peculiarly republican in principle. If republicanism is founded upon good sense, nothing so far removed from good sense can be part and parcel of it. Efficiency is the only just foundation for confidence in a public officer, under republican institutions no less than under monarchs; and short terms which cut off the efficient as surely and inexorably as the inefficient are quite as repugnant to republican as well as monarchical rules of wisdom."

(CG, pages 170–171)

Wilson knew that a better government had to be more efficient.

"The government of a country so vast and various must be strong, prompt, wieldy, and efficient. Its strength must consist in the certainty and uniformity of its purposes, in its accord with national sentiment, in its unhesitating action, and in its honest aims. It must be steadied and approved by open administration diligently obedient to the more permanent judgments of public opinion; and its only active agency, its representative chambers, must be equipped with something besides abundant powers of legislation." (CG, page 206)

In the following chapter, I will sketch out my proposal for how this could be accomplished in our country, in a way that follows both Wilson's critique and our own traditions.

CHAPTER IV

Description of
The New Structure

In the Westminster system, Parliament is a collective term for the three parts of the supreme national authority—the Sovereign (the King or Queen), the House of Lords, and the House of Commons.

Similarly, this new form of our constitution has Congress, the supreme national authority, of three parts: the PRESIDENT as Head of State; the COLLEGE of LEGATES, as representatives of the States; and the HOUSE of REPRESENTATIVES as the supreme legislative authority, with the ADMINISTRATION as a sub-set of the HOUSE, subject to its constant interrogation.

All positions are elective; all amendments are subject to popular vote, as is the Constitution itself.

Note to the reader: I "quilted" this text (found in Appendix I) from a number of sources. The retentions from the U.S. Constitution will be immediately recognized; other sources include the Irish Republic constitution; the Canadian constitution; the New Zealand Constitution Act of 1986, and the Model State Constitution published by the Legislative Drafting Research Fund of Columbia University (1978). The parts not attributable to these sources, most of which are part of the College of Legates section, I wrote in what I hope is in harmony with the rest of these models.

A. The President—Head of State, not Head of Government

Our Head of State will continue to live in the White House, but he (or she) will no longer have the authority of his predecessors. His sole role will be that of the gilded eagle on top of the flagpole of government. The President will sign bills, greet important visitors, and will be the steward of the nation's honor, particularly in his role as Grand Commander of the Order of Honor (that is, the soldiers, sailors and airmen who have earned the Medal of Honor), Grand Commander of the Order of Freedom (those who have been awarded the Medal of Freedom), and any other order Congress chooses to create.

The President will have a term of seven years, with one opportunity to be re-elected. Between three and five candidates will be nominated by the College of Legates. Nominations will be made on the second Monday of January of an election year, elected one month later, and sworn in a month after that. Campaign expenses will be limited to the value of $500,000 (per candidate) as it exists at the time of adoption of the Constitution; the actual dollar amount is therefore indexed for inflation.

The President will be outside the partisan process. He may not be a registered member of a political party, or a lobbyist; neither shall he have made more than nominal contributions to political candidates. I believe this will go a long way to reducing the baneful influence of money-politics in our government.

B. The College of Legates—A Modest Proposal for Non-Partisanship

The College is my proposal to bring to the federal level the tradition of non-partisanship that exists in American political life. It is not in any way analogous to the Senate, for its powers will be completely different.

A significant portion of American electoral politics exists outside the partisan universe. In my home state, New York, as in most states, local boards of education are elected without partisan nomination. In Iowa, local level governments—counties and cities, as well as school districts—are non-partisan. This impressed me when I lived in Iowa. In Nebraska, the entire State Legislature is elected on a non-partisan basis; only the governorship, the other statewide offices, and the Congressional and U.S. Senate seats have partisan elections.

This tradition in American politics, I believe, needs to be represented on the national level. At the same time, a solution will be required for several problems of national government—a solution that needs to be outside the party field. The regular hue and cry that goes up whenever Congress raises its own salary is one such need.

My proposal for the Legates includes:

1. Non-partisan elections, in a similar fashion to the President.
2. Nominated by the Legislatures; elected by the people for a five-year, renewable term.
3. Salaries to be paid by the State or Territory represented by the Legate.
4. Short (five week) electoral process, with campaign expenses severely limited (but, as with the President's campaign, an inflation rider)

5. No other emoluments (e.g., outside speaking fees) allowed while in office.

The College will set the salaries of the Members of the House and the Administration (thus eliminating the Congress-setting-its-own-salary controversy) and will nominate several officers who serve in technical roles in the federal government: an Auditor-General (to run the Congressional Budget Office); a Statistician-General (to run the Census); the Librarian of Congress; the Attorney-General as chief legal adviser to the Government (the nation's top law enforcer—the equivalent to the British Home Secretary—will be in the Cabinet); and the Procurator-General and the United States Attorneys.

The College will also take reapportionment of the House of Representatives out of the partisan process through an independent Boundary Commission similar in the process used in the Commonwealth countries.

The College will screen candidates for Federal judgeships, and will sit, if needed, as a trial Court of Impeachment.

Finally, the College will be the citizen's first resource for hearing complaints against oppression by Federal officials, which has been a central part of the mistrust currently existing between the National Government and its citizens.

C. The House of Representatives

Legislation, administration, and the examination of both will be the exclusive province of the House of Representatives. The College of Legates will have no authority in this field, unlike its analogs in Britain, Ireland, Canada, or Australia.

Representative will be chosen from single-member districts, as under the old Constitution, but the number will be raised from 435 (a Congressionally set arbitrary figure) to between 625 and

650. This is not as fearful as it seems; the United Kingdom, a country much smaller in population than ours, has 650 members in its House of Commons, and the State of New Hampshire's lower house has 400 members. It is also to be recalled that the only speech George Washington made during the Constitutional Convention was a plea for one Representative for every 30,000 persons, instead of one for every 40,000.

An independent boundary commission of the College of Legates will set the boundaries of Representative districts; "gerrymandering" is specifically forbidden. Full voting representatives shall be elected from U.S. territories like Puerto Rico and the U.S. Virgin Islands; after all, Puerto Ricans, Virgin Islanders and other territorial residents are U.S. citizens, and for the first time they will be represented in Congress by voting members of the national legislature.

The maximum term of the House of Representatives shall be four years. This needs to be explained here. If an election takes place on June 1, 2000, the election for the next House of Representatives would have to take place no later than June 1, 2004. However, it could very well take place before that day, through the loss of a vote of no confidence, or the decision of the Prime Minister to choose an earlier date.

Campaign expenses for each Representative candidate will be limited to $10,000 per election per candidate, again indexed for inflation. This is analogous to the law in Britain, where MP candidates' expenses are limited to 4,965 pounds (about $8,000), plus 4.2 pence per elector in urban constituencies or 5.6 pence per elector in rural constituencies. (M.P. candidates also must put up a deposit of 500 pounds, which is forfeited if the candidate does not get a certain fraction of the votes.)

D. The Administration

The section describing the Administration is mostly taken from the constitution of the Republic of Ireland, the only one in which the formation of an Administration or Ministry is written out in usable detail.

The Prime Minister and all others in the Administration must be members of the House of Representatives. The Administration will be collectively responsible for the departments of the Federal Government, and must answer to the House for their actions. The Constitution will require daily questioning of ministers, including the Prime Minister. And the Government may fall at any time if the resolution, "This House has no confidence in the present Administration," passes. Of course, the objective of party organization in the House will be to prevent this, exactly as it happens in the Commonwealth countries.

E. Restrictions Upon Government

Article II collects the Bill of Rights, other Amendments, and the other "no" clauses of the old Constitution, into one compact Article.

Writing these clauses as restrictions upon government, rather than positive assertions of people's rights, is the crown jewel of the "sound sense and practical genius" of the 1787 Constitutional Convention and the First Congress. The authority and duties of the government are derived from the gift of the sovereign people, who in turn were "endowed" with this gift "by their Creator."

A declaration of rights in the form of positive assertions, such as the Universal Declaration of Human Rights, or the Canadian Charter of Rights and Freedoms, assumes that these rights are a gift of government, and can be taken away by the whim of other human beings. Americans rightly reject this conception of their rights, and wonder why other cultures and peoples acquiesce in the potential for having their rights snatched away.

F. The Judiciary

Article III is based on Article III of the old Constitution, but with two changes; the impeachment clauses are consolidated here, rather than spread over several Articles of the old version, and the power of judicial review is severely limited.

It has been a sad feature of our present life that our courts have taken upon themselves the role of legislators. Even U.S. District Courts have presumed upon themselves the authority to void laws passed by Congress.

Even worse, there have been occasions where a U.S. District Court judge in Maine voids a law, and another District Court judge in California upholds the same law, sometimes citing the same sources for opposing decisions.

Furthermore, in no case are any of these decisions subject to examination by anyone, except other judges. They rule by fiat and are a law unto themselves, and unexamined and unjustified at that.

The writers of Eamon de Valera's Irish Constitution of 1937 devised a solution to this impasse. I have incorporated it as Section 5 of Article III. The President, after consulting the Administration and the College of Legates, may refer to the Supreme Court any law or bill (the Irish version applies to bills only) whose constitutionality is questioned. After oral argument, the Supreme Court renders a decision—one only; dissents, if any, are not published. Declarations of constitutionality are reserved to the Supreme Court; all other courts are forbidden to make constitutional rulings.

This is designed to keep the debate and resolution of issues in the legislative and political arena, where they can be resolved by persons responsible to the people, instead of judges responsible to no one.

G. Amending Procedure

"It would seem that no impulse short of the impulse of self-preservation, no force less than the force of revolution, can nowadays be expected to move the cumbrous machinery of formal amendment erected in Article Five," wrote Woodrow Wilson in *Congressional Government* (page 163).

New machinery is needed to replace the "cumbrous" original. The form I have devised in Article IV would place the ultimate decision on amendments to the people in the form of a national referendum.

Amendments will be proposed by the President on recommendation of the Administration, or recommended by the College of Legates or the State Legislatures—unless the Administration objects. The President would fix a Sunday for the national referendum between four and six months ahead of his proclamation. The amendment would have to carry both a majority of the vote overall and a majority of the States. This is to ensure that amendments have a national consensus.

H. Other Highlights

Passage of the Constitution, like passage of amendments, will be by national referendum. However, passage of the Constitution will require the approval of sixty percent of the votes cast, and three-fifths of the states approving.

This follows the precedent of the 1787 Constitution. The Convention had been authorized only to amend the Articles of Confederation, which demanded the unanimous approval of the

13 states. The Convention Fathers bypassed this, declaring that their constitution would go into force upon the approval of nine of the 13 states, thus exceeding their mandate. This new form short-circuits the Article Five amending procedures and puts the ultimate question to the people.

Elections for the House of Representatives, the College of Legates, the President, and for Amendments will be set for Sundays. This draws upon the experience of most continental European countries. Sunday voting allows for greater participation by the electorate, which does not have to balance the need to work with the need to vote. In addition, it would be appropriate that citizens would offer "prayers for those in authority," in the words of the Apostle Peter, during the weekend of the election.

A transitional passage (V.8a, b), derived from the 1937 Irish constitution, upholds the validity of laws during the transition period, should the new document be approved.

CHAPTER V

Responsible Government on The State Level: A Recent History

A. California—Senator Alquist's Proposal

Dissatisfied with the constant gridlock in State Government of California, the senior Member of the Senate of California, Alfred Alquist of San Jose, proposed a Responsible Government constitution for the Golden State in 1994. He submitted a draft to the Senate Committee on Constitutional Amendments, which held a hearing on his draft on 8 March 1995.

Senator Alquist did not submit a brand new constitution; instead, he proposed to re-write fourteen articles of the existing California Constitution to achieve his goal.

His proposal differed from the customs of British parliamentary precedent in a number of ways:

- He did not make the distinction between Head of State and Head of Government that is always made in the Westminster system. Instead, the Governor, as the Senator commanding the majority of the Senate, would be both the "prime minister" and head of state.

- Though Alquist introduced the concept of a *maximum* term, rather than a fixed term for the legislature, he retained the provision on term limits for members of the Legislature that had been voted into the California Constitution by initiative some years earlier. This is in contrast to Woodrow Wilson's observation that "short terms which cut off the efficient as surely and inexorably as the inefficient are quite as repugnant to republican as well as monarchical rules of wisdom." (CG, p. 171) This would have produced the potential for a problem—if there were two "snap" elections in quick succession, all of the members would have been ineligible for the second election, and an entirely new legislature would have to be elected, and no one with any experience of executive government would have been eligible to run.

Alquist also introduced another provision in his draft, unrelated to Westminster structure, that probably killed the proposal. Article XIII, Section 2 allows the Legislature to tax notes, stocks, bonds, deeds of trust, or mortgages, but the rate "shall not exceed four-tenths of one percent of full value," and that the "the tax per dollar of full value shall not be higher on personal property than on real property in the same taxing jurisdiction."

Alquist's proposal was that the "shall nots" in those provisions be struck out and replaced with "may." Thus, the rate on those financial instruments could have been anything the taxing authority pleased, and it could tax at a higher rate than real property. For this reason, the California Taxpayers' Association opposed Sen. Alquist's proposal.

Though Alquist's Senate Committee on Constitutional Amendments passed the proposal, it did not go any further.

B. Minnesota—Jesse Goes to the Mat for a Single House

Surprising all political watchers, former professional wrestler Jesse "The Body" Ventura was elected Governor of Minnesota in 1998. Everyone knew that the Ventura administration was going to be a different kind of government, and there was no disappointment on that score.

Though Gov. Ventura drew the most interest nationwide with talk of a Presidential run on the Reform Party ticket, his widest-ranging state-wide proposal was his advocacy of a single-house, non-partisan legislature for Minnesota. In a policy statement dated 17 August 1999, Gov. Ventura said:

"Our current two-house system lacks accountability. Legislators are able to use the other legislative bodies to justify why a bill did or didn't pass. Under this system, people don't know whom to hold accountable for bad decisions. A single house legislature will require legislators to be responsible for their votes. Every vote will have real consequences, and as a result, legislators will carefully weigh issues rather than simply fall in line behind their caucus.

"…Major policy decisions will no longer be made by a handful of legislators serving on conference committees, notorious for their last-minute, behind-the-scene deals in the dead of night. Professional lobbyists will no longer be the only people who understand and follow the legislative process.

"Increase accountability by requiring legislators to be responsible for their vote. No longer will they be able to use the other legislative body to justify why a bill did or didn't pass. Every vote will have real consequences and people will know whom to hold accountable.

"...Citizens will no longer have to track legislation through multiple committee hearings and conference committees. Average people will be able to easily track legislation through a more streamlined process. Every issue, every amendment and every vote will be conducted under the watchful eye of the citizens.

"...Legislative strategy will no longer hinge on getting the most out of conference committee negotiations. Legislation will be crafted with an eye, not for the upcoming conference committee, but for the public good."

Gov. Ventura's statement, which had an excess of rhetoric and a thimbleful of substance, showed clearly that he had not taken Woodrow Wilson into consideration. Recall that Wilson said that "the piecing of authority, the cutting of it into small bits, which is contrived in our constitutional system," was the heart of the problem. Ventura's proposal, instead of increasing cooperation, would decrease it. Instead two (or three) political parties, each legislator, the governor, each of the other state-wide elected officials, and each judge of the state Supreme Court would be, in effect, a separate political party. The executive would still not be responsible to the legislative branch at all.

Taking my life into my own hands, and making sure that my health insurance was fully paid up, I sent an e-mail message to the Governor, pointing out these flaws, and suggesting that a better way would be a system where responsibility would be transparent—in other words, Responsible Government.

Following my principle of not merely criticizing a proposal, but outlining on what lines it should be replaced, I wrote a draft State Constitution for Minnesota. The Gopher State has a well-written, comprehensible state constitution that was most recently amended by the people in 1998. I took that draft, replaced the clauses on the legislative and executive branches with provisions taken from my New Form U. S. Constitution, and thus came up with a serviceable draft of a Model State Constitution for Responsible Government, which is included in this book as Appendix II.

In order to make the draft reasonably generic, so that Responsible Government proponents could use it in any state, I omitted from it any mention of the State of Minnesota. I also left out a number of provisions specific to the Gopher State, most notably the sections on taconite mining (taconite is a type of iron ore that is principally found in Minnesota but is rare in the other states). Of course, Minnesotans would have the right to fit those provisions back in if they saw fit.

Thus prompted, a model for Responsible Government exists not only for the nation, but for the states as well. As long as the separation of powers model exists on the state level, the shirking of responsibility will happen in the state capitals as well as in Washington. In New York State, where for many years the State Legislature has been split between the Republican-controlled Senate and the Democratic-controlled Assembly, and the Governor has to, by necessity, be from one or the other party, the state budget has missed its constitutional April 1 deadline for more than fifteen years. Frequently, a New York State budget isn't passed until the Fourth of July. California has a June 1 budget deadline in its constitution, and that has frequently been missed—Alquist cited this as one reason for his Responsible Government proposal.

Cabinet government, responsible government, can work on the state level. Clearly the separation of powers model which now prevails has not worked, as shown by the examples cited above, and many others. There is a better way. My wish is that the American people would consider this idea, take up the torch for it in the fifty state capitals, and begin anew the constitutional history of our country.

Conclusion

Submitted for Your Considertaion

The labors you are reading on these pages are the distillation of many years of contemplation about the state of the political institutions of our country. The form I have devised is the combination of my study, my reflection, and my observation of the political situation. As I described earlier, my convictions concerning the superiority of Westminster form of government were formed many years ago. Everything that has happened in politics in the United States since then has reinforced my conviction. The political history of the 1998–1999 period has crystallized my desire to reduce these thoughts to written form and publish them to my fellow citizens.

As a Christian person I am compelled to believe that a "perfect" system of governance cannot be devised by human beings, but is limited to the hope of the new creation. Recent history confirms this belief. Therefore, this new constitutional structure is not "perfect." Nevertheless, I sincerely believe that the Westminster system is the best system that fallible man can produce. I hope that I have demonstrated that in any event the proximate cause of the ills that plague our country is our structure of governance, and that our country needs to take a deep look inside itself and decide that continuing this structure will only lead to further disasters.

I produced this work because I hope in the future in our country. The protest generation of "the sixties" believed in destruction, both personal and political. This opinion is amply documented. I wanted to show my country a new way to self-governance, because the present way is no government. The dogs in an Iditarod sled team have more responsibility than our government. The dogs all run in one direction, otherwise the sled goes nowhere; our government can go in five hundred and thirty-six directions at once. Is it any wonder we are going nowhere? With this system, we have the possibility of going somewhere, and fixing responsibility for the path we take.

The "constitution" of our country is more than a written document; it contains everything of value, everything that is good, true, and noble in the American culture and experience. Abandoning a failed structure of government will not destroy our "constitution," because it is now more that just the words that the Founders set down on ink and parchment in Philadelphia in 1787. Our commitment to "the proposition that all men are created equal"; our commitment to principle that all human beings "are endowed by their Creator with certain inalienable rights"; our commitment to "government of the people, by the people, for the people"; our commitment to the rule of law anchored on authentic truth—that commitment is the real Constitution of the United States.

PATRICK J. McGRATH, Jr.
Stony Point, New York
January 1999—January 2000

Appendix I

The Constitution of The United States —New Form

Preamble

Article I—STRUCTURE AND FUNCTIONS OF GOVERNMENT

A. The President
B. The College of Legates
C. The House of Representatives
D. The Administration
Article II—RESTRICTIONS UPON GOVERNMENT
Article III—THE JUDICIARY
Article IV—PROCEDURE OF AMENDMENT
Article V—TRANSITORY AND MISCELLANEOUS PROVISIONS

WE THE PEOPLE OF THE UNITED STATES,

IN ORDER TO FORM A MORE PERFECT UNION, ESTABLISH JUSTICE, INSURE DOMESTIC TRANQUILITY, PROVIDE FOR THE COMMON DEFENCE, PROMOTE THE

GENERAL WELFARE, AND SECURE THE BLESSINGS OF LIBERTY TO OURSELVES AND OUR POSTERITY, DO ORDAIN AND ESTABLISH IN THIS NEW FORM THIS

CONSTITUTION FOR
THE UNITED STATES OF AMERICA.

ARTICLE I—STRUCTURE AND FUNCTIONS OF GOVERNMENT

The people of the United States, reserving to themselves the right "to institute new government…as to them shall seem most likely to effect their safety and happiness," vest their sovereign authority in the Congress of the United States, which shall be deemed to consist of: the President of the United States, the College of States' Legates, and the House of Representatives.

A. THE PRESIDENT OF THE UNITED STATES

1. The authority of the head of state shall be vested in the office of President of the United States.

2. The President of the United States shall be chosen in the following manner:

　a. The College of Legates shall sit in Convention on the second Monday in January following the adoption of this Constitution, and the second Monday of January every seventh year following, for the sole purpose of proposing to the people candidates for President of the United States.

　b. The College shall nominate at least two but no more than five candidates for the Presidency. The College shall determine by its own rules how nominations shall be accomplished.

c. On the first Sunday in February following nominations by the College, the people shall elect one of the persons nominated as President of the United States. The candidate receiving the most votes shall be declared elected.

3. The person elected President of the United States shall be sworn into office on the first Monday in March following the election. Upon inauguration the President-elect shall make the following oath or affirmation:

"I, N., do solemnly swear (or affirm) that I will faithfully execute the office of President of the United States, and will to the best of my Ability, preserve, protect, and defend the Constitution of the United States."

4. The following shall be the qualifications for the Presidency:

a. Attainment of the age of 40 years;

b. Registration as a voter in the candidate's State of residence;

c. Not being registered as a member of a political party;

d. Not being a member or a former member of the committee of any political party;

e. Not being a lobbyist, defined by common usage of the term or by an Act of Congress;

f. Not having contributed more than $500 to any political candidate in the ten years before the nomination;

g. Not currently holding any office of profit or trust under the United States, or any of them, or any State subdivision, except as provided below.

5. Former members of the House of Representatives or of the College of Legates shall be eligible for nomination, but the provisions of subsections a., b., e., and f., of Section 4 above shall still apply.

6. The incumbent President shall be eligible for re-nomination, but only once.

7. Campaign expenses for the Presidency shall be limited to the value of $500,000 per candidate as it existed at the time of the adoption of this Constitution, unless provided for otherwise by Act of Congress.

8. In case of the Removal of the President from Office, or of the President's Death, Resignation, or Inability to discharge the Powers and Duties of his Office, the same shall devolve upon the Chancellor of the College of Legates, who shall take the oath of the Presidency, become President, and complete the balance of the incumbent term; any further provision on this question shall be regulated by Act of Congress.

9. The President shall receive at stated Times receive for his Services, a Compensation, which shall be neither increased nor diminished during the Period for which he shall be elected, and he shall not receive within that period any other Emolument from the United States, or any of them.

10 a. The President shall be Commander-in-Chief of the Armed Forces of the United States, but will act in this capacity only on the advice of the appropriate Minister of State;

b. He may require the Opinion, in writing, of the principal Officer in each of the executive Departments, upon any Subject relating to the Duties of their respective Offices;

c. He shall have the Power, subject to the advice of the appropriate Minister of State, to grant Reprieves and Pardons for Offenses against the United States, except in cases of Impeachment;

d. He shall ratify Treaties, upon the advice of the appropriate Minister of State;

e. He shall appoint, upon the advice of the appropriate Minister of State, Ambassadors, other diplomatic Ministers, and Consuls, and all other Officers of the United States, whose Appointments are not herein otherwise provided for: but Congress may by Law vest the appointment of such inferior Officers, as they think proper, in the Courts of Law, or in the Heads of Departments.

f. He shall at the beginning of each session of Congress present an Address on the State of the Union, in which Address the President, on the advice of the Administration, shall recommend to their consideration such measures as he considers necessary and expedient, and give notice of the Estimates for the Public Service to be laid before the House; to which Address the House of Representatives shall debate and vote a Reply.

g. He may, on extraordinary occasions, convene the College of Legates or the House of Representatives, or both.

h. He shall dissolve the House of Representatives and order new elections to the House on the advice of the Prime Minister, though he may in his absolute discretion, refuse to dissolve the House on the advice of a Prime Minister who has ceased to retain the support of a majority of the House of Representatives.

i. He shall receive Ambassadors and other diplomatic Ministers; he shall take care that the Laws shall be faithfully executed, and shall Commission all the Officers of the United States.

j. He shall be, by virtue of his Office

- Grand Commander of the Order of Honor, for holders of the Medal of Honor;

- Grand Commander of the Order of Freedom, for holders of the Medal of Freedom;

- Grand Commander of any order of Honor and Service that shall be established by Congress.

11. A Bill passed by the House of Representatives shall become law when the President assents to it, upon the advice of the Prime Minister, and signs it in token of such assent.

12. The powers conferred upon the President shall be exercised by him only upon the advice of the Administration.

B. THE COLLEGE OF STATES' LEGATES

1. The supervision of the Federal Government on behalf of the States shall be vested in the College of States' Legates, also known as the College of Legates.

2. The College shall consist of two Legates from each State, and one Legate each from the District of Columbia, Puerto Rico, the U.S. Virgin Islands, Guam, American Samoa, and any other Possession of the United States so designated by Act of Congress.

3. On the first Monday in January following the adoption of this Constitution, and every fifth year thereafter, the Legislatures of the several States and Territories shall sit in their respective capitals in joint session for the purpose of nominating candidates as Legates of their respective States and Territories.

a. Each Legislature shall establish its own rules for nominations to the Legateship.

b. Each State Legislature shall nominate at least four, but no more than seven candidates; each Territorial Legislature shall nominate at least three but no more than five candidates.

4. On the second Sunday following the nomination, the people shall vote in their States and Territories for their Legates—two per State, one from each of the designated Territories. The two candidates receiving the most votes (or the one candidate in the Territory) shall be elected Legates.

5. On the second Monday following the election, the Legates shall proceed to their respective capitals, where they shall subscribe the following oath from the Executive Authority thereof:

"I, N., do solemnly swear (or affirm) that I will faithfully execute the high office of Legate, and will to the best of my ability, preserve, protect, and defend the Constitution of the United States."

6. On the Monday following taking their oaths, the Legates shall assemble in the national capital, under the temporary presidency of a Delegate of the President, and shall proceed

immediately to the election of one of their number as Chancellor of the College and another as Vice-Chancellor.

7. When a year occurs that the election of the President and the election of Legates coincide, the election of Legates shall begin on the first Monday of March, and proceed in the same fashion as if it took place on the first Monday in January.

8. The Legates shall receive for their Services a Compensation, to be paid out of the Treasuries of their respective States or Territories, which compensation shall not be increased nor decreased during their terms of office.

> a. The States and Territories may, if they wish, agree on a common rate of compensation for Legates, but no State or Territory shall be compelled to agree to this.
>
> b. The Legates shall not receive any other compensation for anything else, other than income from previous or current investments, during their term of office.
>
> c. Persons employed by the College of Legates shall be compensated from the Treasury of the United States.

9. Candidates for the College of Legates shall have the following qualifications:

> a. They shall have attained to the full age of Thirty-Five years;
>
> b. They shall be registered voters of the State or Territory they represent;
>
> c. They shall not be registered members of any political party, as defined by the laws of their respective State or Territory, or, if political affiliation is not declared at registration, shall not be members of the committee of any political party;

d. They shall not be lobbyists as defined by the common meaning of the word or by applicable law;

e. They shall not have made a contribution of more than $100 to any one political candidate, nor more than $1000 altogether, in the five years prior to their election;

f. They shall currently hold no office of profit or trust of the United States, or any of them, or their subdivisions.

10. Incumbent Legates are eligible for re-election.

11. Campaign expenses for candidates to the College of Legates shall be limited by law but in no case shall exceed the value of $20,000 (per candidate) as it existed at the adoption of this Constitution.

12. No bill, order, vote, or resolution of the House of Representatives shall be in order for consideration by the College of Legates.

13. The Authority of the College of Legates shall extend to:

a. The nomination of candidates for the Presidency, in accordance with the provisions of this Constitution;

b. The appointment of a Committee of Legates as a Boundary Commission for seats in the House of Representatives;

c. The appointment of an Auditor-General, who shall head the accounting office of Congress as provided by law;

d. The appointment of a Statistician-General, who shall be in charge of the decennial Census and the other statistical functions of the Federal Government, as provided by law;

e. The appointment of the Librarian of Congress;

f. The appointment of the Attorney-General of the United States as chief legal adviser to the Government;

g. The appointment of the Procurator-General of the United States, and the chief prosecutors of the judicial districts of the United States;

h. The appointment of a Committee of Legates as a Screening Committee to recommend to the Administration appointments to Federal judgeships;

i. The examination into complaints from citizens of the United States of wrongdoing by officials of the United States, and the exposure and public humiliation of any public official committing any act of wrongdoing against any private person, for which the College shall have the power of subpoena, and if criminal wrongdoing shall be found, shall refer the matter for prosecution to the appropriate authorities;

j. The authority to recommend to the House of Representatives a scale of compensation and benefits for the President, the Representatives, the Prime Minister, the Ministers of State, the Leader of the Opposition, the Shadow Ministers, the Whips and the other Leaders of Caucus, and the Judges of the United States; the House of Representatives may accept or reject their recommendation but may not alter it on its own motion;

k. The authority to pass resolutions expressing the sense of the College on any matter, these resolutions being understood to have no force of law;

l. Any authority delegated to it by Act of Congress, which may be withdrawn at any time by another Act of Congress.

14. The College shall determine the Rules of its Proceedings, punish Members for disorderly conduct, and, with the concurrence of two-thirds of the whole College, expel a Member and request that the Legislature of the State concerned immediately appoint a successor to fill out the term of the expelled Legate.

15. The College shall keep a verbatim Journal of its proceedings and publish it from time to time, excepting such parts as may in its Judgment require Secrecy, and the Yeas and Nays of the Legates on any question, on the request of one-fifth of the members present, shall be entered in the Journal.

C. THE HOUSE OF REPRESENTATIVES

1. All legislative powers herein granted to Congress shall be vested in the House of Representatives.

2 a. The House of Representatives shall consist of Members chosen by the people of the United States.

b. The House shall consist between of 625 and 650 Members, with one Representative returned from each district.

c. A committee of the College of Legates shall propose a plan after each decennial census for the re-apportionment of the House of Representatives. The House shall approve or disapprove of the plan as it sees fit, but may not alter the plan on its own motion.

d. Each State shall be represented by at least one Representative.

e. Each Territory shall be represented by at least one Representative, and such additional Representatives in proportion to its population.

f. The apportionment plan shall divide the United States into as many districts as there are Representatives. The districts shall consist of compact and contiguous territory. All districts shall be so nearly equal in population that the population of the smallest does not vary from the population of the largest by more than five per cent.

g. Each Representative district shall fall within the boundaries of one state or territory.

3 a. No person shall be a representative who shall not have attained to the age of twenty-five years, and been seven years a citizen of the United States.

b. Campaign expenses for candidates to the House of Representatives shall be limited by law but in no case shall exceed the value of $10,000 (per candidate) as it exists at the time of the adoption of this Constitution.

4. When vacancies occur in the House, the Speaker shall promptly issue writs of election to fill such vacancies.

5. The President of the United States shall from Time to Time, by instrument under the Great Seal of the United States, summon and call together the House of Representatives.

6. A member of the College of Legates shall not be capable of being elected or of sitting or voting as a member of the House of Representatives.

7. The House of Representatives shall, at its first meeting after any general election of its members, and immediately after any

vacancy occurs in the office of Speaker, choose one of its members as Speaker, and every such choice shall be effective on being confirmed by the President.

8. The Speaker shall preside at all sittings of the House, and the House shall provide, by its own rules, for the case of the absence of the Speaker for more than forty-eight hours.

9. A Representative shall not be permitted to sit or vote in the House until he has sworn or affirmed the following oath before the President or a person authorized by him to administer the oath:

> "I, N., do solemnly swear (or affirm) that I shall faithfully execute the office of Representative, and will to the best of my ability, preserve, protect, and defend the Constitution of the United States."

10. Every House of Representatives shall continue for Four Years from the day of the Return of the Writs for choosing the House, and no longer, subject to being sooner dissolved by the President.

11. After any general election, the House shall meet no later than four weeks after the day fixed for the Return of the Writs of that election.

12. It shall not be lawful for the House to adopt or pass any Vote, Resolution, Address, or Bill for Appropriation of any Part of the Public Revenue, or of any Tax or Impost, to any purpose that has not been recommended by Message of the President in the Session in which such Vote, Resolution, Address, or Bill for Appropriation is proposed.

13. It shall not be lawful for Congress, except by or under an Act of Congress:

—to levy a tax;

—to raise a loan or receive any money as a loan from
  any person;

—or to spend any public money.

14. The House shall be the Judge of the Elections, Returns, and Qualifications of its Members, and a Majority shall constitute a Quorum to do Business; but a smaller Number may adjourn from day to day and may be authorized to compel the attendance of absent Members, in such manner and under such Penalties as the House may provide.

15. The House may determine the Rules of its Proceedings, punish Members for disorderly Behavior, and, with the concurrence of two-thirds, expel a Member.

16. The House shall keep a verbatim Journal of its proceedings, and shall from time to time publish it, excepting such parts as may in its judgment require Secrecy; and the Yeas and Nays of the Members of the House on any question shall, at the desire of one-fifth of those present, be entered on the Journal.

17. Representatives and Legates shall in all Cases, except Treason, Felony, and Breach of the Peace, be privileged from Arrest during their attendance at the Session of their respective Houses, and in going to and returning from the same; and for any speech or debate in either House, they shall not be questioned in any other place.

18. No law shall be passed except by bill and no bill except bills for appropriations and bills for the codification, rearrangement, or revision of existing laws, shall have more than one subject.

19. No bill shall become a law unless it has been printed and in the designated mailboxes of the members in final form at least three days prior to final passage, and the majority of all the members has assented to it. The yeas and nays on final passage shall be entered into the journal and published.

20. The House of Representatives may establish such committees it shall deem necessary for the conduct of its business. These committees shall be governed by Rules established by the House.

21. The House shall assemble at least once in every year, and such meeting shall begin at noon on the second Monday of January, unless they shall by law appoint a different day.

22. The Congress shall have Power

- To lay and collect Taxes, Duties, Imposts and Excises, to pay the Debts and provide for the common Defence and general Welfare of the United States; but all Duties, Imposts, and Excises shall be uniform throughout the United States;

- To borrow Money on the credit of the United States;

- To regulate Commerce with foreign Nations, and among the several States, and with the Indian Tribes;

- To establish a uniform Rule of Naturalization, and uniform Laws on the subject of Bankruptcies throughout the United States;

- To coin Money, regulate the Value thereof, and of foreign Coin, and fix the standard of Weights and Measures;

- To provide for the Punishment of counterfeiting the Securities and current Coin of the United States;

- To establish Post Offices and post Roads;

- To promote the Progress of Science and useful Arts, by securing for limited Times to Authors and Inventors the exclusive Right to their respective Writings and Discoveries;

- To constitute Tribunals inferior to the supreme Court;

- To define and punish Piracies and Felonies committed on the high Seas, and Offenses against the Law of Nations;

- To declare War, grant Letters of Marque and Reprisal, and make Rules concerning Captures on Land and Water;

- To raise and support Armies, but no Appropriation of Money to that Use shall be for a longer term than two Years;

- To provide and maintain a Navy;

- To make Rules for the Government and Regulation of the land and naval Forces;

- To provide for the organizing, arming, and disciplining, the Militia, and for governing such Part of them as may be employed in the Service of the United States, reserving to the States respectively, the Appointment of the Officers, and the Authority of training the Militia according to the discipline prescribed by Congress;

- To exercise exclusive Legislation in all Cases whatsoever, over such District (not exceeding ten Miles square) as may, by Cession of particular States, and the Acceptance of Congress, become the Seat of Government of the United States, and to exercise like Authority over all Places purchased by the Consent of the Legislature of the State in which the Same shall be, for the Erection of Forts, Magazines, Arsenals, dock-Yards and other needful Buildings;

- And to make all Laws which shall be necessary and proper for carrying into Execution the foregoing Powers, and all other Powers vested by this Constitution in the Government of the United States, or in any Department or Officer thereof.

D. THE ADMINISTRATION

1. The executive Powers of Congress shall be governed by the Administration.

2. The Administration shall consist of the Prime Minister and such other Ministers of State as the President, on the advice of the Prime Minister, shall appoint.

3. The head of the Administration shall be called, and in this Constitution is referred to as the Prime Minister.

4 a. The President shall grant the Seals of the Office of Prime Minister to that Member of the House of Representatives who commands the Majority of the House.

b. The President shall grant the Seal of Office of a Ministry of State to any Representative whom the Prime Minister designates; the President shall withdraw the seals of a minister on the advice of the Prime Minister.

5. No Person shall be granted the Seals of Office of Prime Minister or Minister of State unless he is also a Member of the House of Representatives.

6. The Administration shall be collectively responsible for the Federal Departments of State.

7. The Administration each year shall prepare Estimates of the Receipts and Expenditures of the Public Service, and shall lay these Estimates for consideration by the House.

8. a. The Prime Minister may resign at any time by surrendering the Seals of Office to the President.

   b. Any member of the Administration may resign by surrendering the Seals of Office to the Prime Minister for submission to the President.

   c. The President shall accept the resignation of a member of the Administration, other than the Prime Minister, if so advised by the Prime Minister.

   d. The Members of the Administration in office at the date of the dissolution of the House shall continue to hold office until their successors are appointed.

9. It shall be in order at any time for the Leader of the Official Opposition to lay before the House the motion, "This House has no confidence in the present Administration," and if the motion shall pass, the Administration shall resign, and the Prime Minister shall request that the President dissolve the House and issue writs for a new election, as provided in this Constitution.

10. During each day's sitting of the House, at least one hour shall be devoted to questioning Ministers of State on the performance of their duties; at least 40 minutes a week shall be reserved for questioning the Prime Minister or his designated representative.

ARTICLE II—RESTRICTIONS UPON GOVERNMENT

The people, holding to the self-evident truth that all human beings "are endowed by their Creator with certain inalienable rights," place the following restrictions upon Government:

1. No law shall be made respecting an establishment of religion, or prohibiting the free exercise thereof.

2. No law shall be made abridging the freedom of speech, or of the Press.

3. No law shall be made abridging the right of the people peaceably to assemble, and to petition the Government for a redress of grievances.

4. The Privilege of the Writ of Habeas Corpus shall not be suspended, unless when in cases of Rebellion or Invasion the public Safety may require it.

5. No Bill of Attainder or ex post facto law shall be passed.

6. No Tax or Duty shall be laid on articles exported from any State

7. No Preference shall be given by any Regulation of Commerce or Revenue to the Ports of one State over those of another; nor shall Vessels bound to, or from, one State, be obliged to enter, clear, or pay Duties in another.

8. No Title of Nobility shall be granted by the United States; and no Person holding an office of Profit or Trust under them shall, without the consent of Congress, accept of any Present, Emolument, Office, or Title, of any kind whatsoever, from any King, Prince, or Foreign State.

9. No State shall enter into any Treaty, Alliance, or Confederation; grant Letters of Marque and Reprisal; coin Money; emit Bills of Credit; make any Thing but gold and silver Coin a Tender in Payment of Debts; pass any Bill of Attainder, ex post facto Law, or Law impairing the obligation of Contracts, or grant any Title of Nobility.

10. No State shall, without the consent of Congress, lay any Imposts or Duties except what may be absolutely necessary for executing its inspection Laws: and the net Produce of all Duties and Imposts, laid by any State on Imports and Exports, shall be

for the Use of the Treasury of the United States; and all such laws shall be subject to the Revision and Control of Congress.

11. No State shall, without the consent of Congress, lay any Duty of Tonnage, keep Troops, or Ships of War in time of Peace, enter into any Agreement or Compact with another State, or with a foreign Power, or engage in War, unless actually invaded, or in such imminent Danger as will not admit of delay.

12. No religious test shall ever be required as a Qualification to any Office or Public Trust under the United States.

13. A well-regulated Militia, being necessary to the security of a free State, the right of the people to keep and bear Arms, shall not be infringed.

14. No Soldier shall, in time of peace be quartered in any house, without the consent of the Owner, nor in time of War, but in a manner to be prescribed by law.

15. The right of the people to be secure in their persons, houses, papers, and effects, against unreasonable searches and seizures, shall not be violated, and no Warrants shall issue, but upon probable cause, supported by Oath or affirmation, and particularly describing the place to be searched, and the persons or things to be seized.

16. No person shall be held to answer for a capital, or otherwise infamous crime, unless on a presentment or indictment of a grand jury, except in cases arising in the land or naval forces, or in the militia, when in actual service in time of war or public danger; nor shall any person be subject for the same offense to be twice put in jeopardy of life or limb; nor shall be compelled in any criminal case to be a witness against himself, nor be deprived of life, liberty, or property, without due process of law; nor shall private property be taken for public use, without just compensation.

17. In all criminal prosecutions, the accused shall enjoy the right to a speedy and public trial, by an impartial jury of the state

and district wherein the crime shall have been committed, which district shall have been previously ascertained by law, and to be informed of the nature and cause of the accusation; to be confronted with the witnesses against him; to have compulsory process for obtaining witnesses in his favor, and to have the assistance of counsel for his defense.

18. In suits at common law, where the value in controversy shall exceed one thousand dollars, the right of trial by jury shall be preserved, and no fact tried by a jury, shall be otherwise reexamined in any court of the United States, than according to the rules of the common law.

19. Excessive bail shall not be required, nor excessive fines imposed, nor cruel and unusual punishments inflicted.

20. The enumeration in the Constitution, of certain rights, shall not be construed to deny or disparage others retained by the people.

21. The powers not delegated to the United States by the Constitution, nor prohibited by it to the states, are reserved to the states respectively, or to the people.

22. The judicial power of the United States shall not be construed to extend to any suit in law or equity, commenced or prosecuted against one of the United States by citizens of another state, or by citizens or subjects of any foreign state.

23. Neither slavery nor involuntary servitude, except as a punishment for crime whereof the party shall have been duly convicted, shall exist within the United States, or any place subject to their jurisdiction.

24. All persons born or naturalized in the United States, and subject to the jurisdiction thereof, are citizens of the United States and of the state wherein they reside. No state shall make or enforce any law which shall abridge the privileges or immunities of citizens of the United States; nor shall any state deprive any

person of life, liberty, or property, without due process of law; nor deny to any person within its jurisdiction the equal protection of the laws.

25. No person shall be President of the United States, or a Legate or Representative in Congress, or hold any office, civil or military, under the United States, or under any state, who, having previously taken an oath, as a member of Congress, or as an officer of the United States, or as a member of any state legislature, or as an executive or judicial officer of any state, to support the Constitution of the United States, shall have engaged in insurrection or rebellion against the same, or given aid or comfort to the enemies thereof. But an Act of Congress may remove such disability.

26. The validity of the public debt of the United States, authorized by law, including debts incurred for payment of pensions and bounties for services in suppressing insurrection or rebellion, shall not be questioned. But neither the United States nor any state shall assume or pay any debt or obligation incurred in aid of insurrection or rebellion against the United States, or any claim for the loss or emancipation of any slave; but all such debts, obligations and claims shall be held illegal and void.

27. The right of citizens of the United States to vote shall not be denied or abridged by the United States or by any state on account of race, color, or previous condition of servitude.

28. The right of citizens of the United States to vote shall not be denied or abridged by the United States or by any state on account of sex.

29. The transportation or importation into any state, territory, or possession of the United States for delivery or use therein of intoxicating liquors, in violation of the laws thereof, is hereby prohibited.

30. The right of citizens of the United States to vote in any election for President, or for Legate or Representative in Congress, shall not be denied or abridged by the United States or any state by reason of failure to pay any poll tax or other tax.

31. The right of citizens of the United States, who are 18 years of age or older, to vote, shall not be denied or abridged by the United States or any state on account of age.

ARTICLE III—THE JUDICIARY

1. The judicial power of the United States shall be vested in one supreme Court, and in such inferior courts as the Congress may from time to time ordain and establish. The judges, both of the supreme and inferior courts, shall hold their offices during good behavior, and shall, at stated times, receive for their services, a compensation, which shall not be diminished during their continuance in office.

2 a. The judicial power shall extend to all cases, in law and equity, arising under this Constitution, the laws of the United States, and treaties made, or which shall be made, under their authority; to all cases affecting ambassadors, other public ministers and consuls; to all cases of admiralty and maritime jurisdiction; to controversies to which the United States shall be a party; to controversies between two or more states; between a state and citizens of another state; between citizens of different states; between citizens of the same state claiming lands under grants of different states, and between a state, or the citizens thereof, and foreign states, citizens or subjects.

b. In all cases affecting ambassadors, other public ministers and consuls, and those in which a state shall be party, the Supreme Court shall have original jurisdiction. In all the other cases before mentioned, the Supreme Court shall have appellate jurisdiction, both as to law and fact, with such exceptions, and under such regulations as the Congress shall make.

c. The trial of all crimes, except in cases of impeachment, shall be by jury; and such trial shall be held in the state where the said crimes shall have been committed; but when not committed within any state, the trial shall be at such place or places as the Congress may by law have directed.

3 a. The President, the Judges, and all civil Officers of the United States shall be removed from office on Impeachment for, and Conviction of, Treason, Bribery, or other high Crimes and Misdemeanors.

b. The House of Representatives shall have the sole power of Impeachment, and the College of Legates shall have the sole power to try all Impeachments.

c. When sitting as a Court of Impeachment, the Legates shall be on Oath or Affirmation. When the President of the United States is tried, the Chief Justice shall preside; and no Person shall be convicted without the concurrence of two-thirds of the members present.

d. Judgment in Cases of Impeachment shall not extend further than to removal from office, and disqualification to hold and enjoy any office of honor, trust, or profit under the United States; but the Party convicted shall nevertheless be liable and subject to Indictment, Trial, Judgment and Punishment, according to law.

4 a. Treason against the United States, shall consist only in levying war against them, or in adhering to their enemies, giving them aid and comfort. No person shall be convicted of treason unless on the testimony of two witnesses to the same overt act, or on confession in open court.

b. The Congress shall have power to declare the punishment of treason, but no attainder of treason shall work corruption of blood, or forfeiture except during the life of the person attainted.

5. The Judges of the supreme and inferior courts shall be appointed by the President by writ under the Great Seal of the United States, upon the recommendation of the Prime Minister or other appropriate Minister of State, who shall make recommendations from a list compiled by a Screening Committee of the College of Legates.

6 a. The President may, after consultation with the Administration and the College of Legates, refer any Bill or Law, or any specified provision or provisions of such Bills or Laws, to the Supreme Court for a decision on the question of whether the legislation so referred is repugnant to this Constitution.

b. If a Bill has not yet been signed in token of the President's assent, the President shall not sign it pending the decision of the Court.

c. The Supreme Court, consisting of no fewer than seven judges, shall consider every question referred to it by the President under this article for a decision, and, having heard arguments by or on behalf of the Attorney-General and by counsel assigned by the Court, shall pronounce its decision in open court as soon as may be, but not less than sixty days after the date of such reference.

d. The decision of the majority of the judges of the Supreme Court shall be the decision of the Court and shall be pronounced by one of the judges as the Court shall direct, and no other opinion, whether assenting or dissenting, shall be pronounced, nor shall the existence of any other such opinion be disclosed.

e. A law, or any portion of a law, which the Supreme Court declares repugnant to the Constitution, shall no longer be law, but any portion not so declared shall remain law.

f. In every case in which the Supreme Court decides that any provision of a Bill repugnant to the Constitution, or any provision thereof, the President shall decline to sign it; in every other case, the President shall sign the Bill as soon as may be after the date on which the decision of the Supreme Court shall be pronounced.

g. The Supreme Court has original, exclusive, and final jurisdiction to declare Laws or Bills repugnant to the Constitution; all courts of inferior jurisdiction shall assume that Laws are not so repugnant, absent such pronouncement from the Supreme Court.

ARTICLE IV—PROCEDURE OF AMENDMENT

1 a. Amendments to this Constitution may be proposed from time to time by the President for approval by the people.

b. Amendments shall be proposed by the President on the advice of the Administration.

c. Amendments may also be recommended by a resolution of the College of Legates or on the application of two-thirds of the Legislatures of the States; but the President shall not propose such amendments if the Administration advises against it.

2. An amendment shall be proposed to the people by a writ from the President under the Great Seal of the United States, setting forth the text of the amendment, and the date of its vote for approval, which date shall be a Sunday between four and six months from the date of the writ.

3. The amendment shall have been deemed passed when approved by:

a. A majority of the votes cast overall, and;

b. Majorities of the votes cast in more than one-half of the states.

ARTICLE V—TRANSITORY AND MISCELLANEOUS PROVISIONS

1. Full faith and credit shall be given in each state to the public acts, records, and judicial proceedings of every other state. And the Congress may by general laws prescribe the manner in which such acts, records, and proceedings shall be proved, and the effect thereof.

2. The citizens of each state shall be entitled to all privileges and immunities of citizens in the several states.

3. A person charged in any state with treason, felony, or other crime, who shall flee from justice, and be found in another state, shall on demand of the executive authority of the state from which he fled, be delivered up, to be removed to the state having jurisdiction of the crime.

4. New states may be admitted by the Congress into this union; but no new states shall be formed or erected within the jurisdiction of any other state; nor any state be formed by the junction of two or more states, or parts of states, without the consent of the legislatures of the states concerned as well as of the Congress.

5. The Congress shall have power to dispose of and make all needful rules and regulations respecting the territory or other property belonging to the United States; and nothing in this Constitution shall be so construed as to prejudice any claims of the United States, or of any particular state.

6. The United States shall guarantee to every state in this union a republican form of government, and shall protect each of them against invasion; and on application of the legislature, or of the executive (when the legislature cannot be convened) against domestic violence.

7. All debts contracted and engagements entered into, before the adoption of this Constitution, shall be as valid against the United States under this Constitution, as under the Confederation.

8 a. Subject to this Constitution, and to the extent that they are not inconsistent therewith, the laws of the United States immediately prior to the date of the coming into operation of this Constitution shall continue to be of full force and effect until the laws or

any of them shall have been repealed or amended by an Act of Congress.

b. Laws enacted before, but expressed to come into force after the coming into operation of this Constitution shall, unless otherwise enacted by Act of Congress, come into force in accordance with the terms thereof.

9 a. This Constitution shall come into force after having been proposed to the people by the President of the United States of the old form of this Constitution, and approved by the people by referendum set by the President for a Sunday between six and twelve months after the President proposes it by writ under the Great Seal of the United States.

b. Approval shall have been granted if this Constitution receives the "Yes" votes of sixty percent of the votes cast throughout the United States, and a majority of votes in three-fifths of the states.

10. This Constitution shall come into force on the second January 1 or July 1 following approval of this Constitution by the people, whichever is the later of the two.

11. If this Constitution is approved by the people, the Congress of the old form of this constitution shall pass transitory laws to assist the effect of this constitution, including, but not limited to, creating an impartial boundary commission for the creation of new legislative district boundaries, and fixing the date for elections to the new House of Representatives; but no transitory law passed by the Congress of the old form of this constitution shall be repugnant to this Constitution in the new form.

12. This Constitution, and the laws of the United States which shall be made in pursuance thereof; and all treaties made, or which shall be made, under the authority of the United States, shall be the supreme law of the land; and the judges in every state shall be bound thereby, anything in the Constitution or laws of any State to the contrary notwithstanding.

Appendix II

Model State Constitution for Responsible Government

Produced by
The Campaign for Responsible Government

Based on the Constitution of the State of Minnesota
as amended to 1998
and on the
Model U.S. Constitution
of the Campaign for Responsible Government

Note to our Minnesota friends: Since this is meant to be a generic constitution with applicability to any state, we have left out provisions that only apply to Minnesota, such as the taconite mining provisions. Of course, a real draft final draft for Minnesota may leave in such provisions, as the people see fit.

Preamble

We, the people of this state, grateful to God for our civil and religious liberty, and desiring to perpetuate its blessings and secure the same to ourselves and our posterity, do ordain and establish this Constitution.

Article I. Bill of rights.

Article II. Name and boundaries.

Article III. Structure and functions of Government

Article IV. Judiciary.

Article V. Elective franchise.

Article VI. Impeachment and removal from office.

Article VII. Amendment to the constitution.

Article VIII. Taxation.

Article IX. Appropriations and finances.

Article X. Special legislation; local government.

Article XI. Miscellaneous subjects.

Article XII. Public highway system.

ARTICLE I—BILL OF RIGHTS

Section 1. OBJECT OF GOVERNMENT. Government is instituted for the security, benefit and protection of the people, in whom all political power is inherent, together with the right to alter, modify or reform government whenever required by the public good.

Sec. 2. RIGHTS AND PRIVILEGES. No member of this state shall be disfranchised or deprived of any of the rights or privileges secured to any citizen thereof, unless by the law of the land or the judgment of his peers. There shall be neither slavery nor involuntary servitude in the state otherwise than as punishment for a crime of which the party has been convicted.

Sec. 3. LIBERTY OF THE PRESS. The liberty of the press shall forever remain inviolate, and all persons may freely speak, write and publish their sentiments on all subjects, being responsible for the abuse of such right.

Sec. 4. TRIAL BY JURY. The right of trial by jury shall remain inviolate, and shall extend to all cases at law without regard to the amount in controversy. A jury trial may be waived by the parties in all cases in the manner prescribed by law. The legislature may provide that the agreement of five-sixths of a jury in a civil action or proceeding, after not less than six hours' deliberation, is a sufficient verdict. The legislature may provide for the number of jurors in a civil action or proceeding, provided that a jury have at least six members.

Sec. 5. NO EXCESSIVE BAIL OR UNUSUAL PUNISH-MENTS. Excessive bail shall not be required, nor excessive fines imposed, nor cruel or unusual punishments inflicted.

Sec. 6. RIGHTS OF ACCUSED IN CRIMINAL PROSECU-TIONS. In all criminal prosecutions the accused shall enjoy the right to a speedy and public trial by an impartial jury of the county or district wherein the crime shall have been committed, which county or district shall have been previously ascertained by law. In all prosecutions of crimes defined by law as felonies, the accused has the right to a jury of 12 members. In all other criminal prosecutions, the legislature may provide for the number of jurors, provided that a jury have at least six members. The accused shall enjoy the right to be informed of the nature and cause of the accusation, to be confronted with the witnesses against him, to have compulsory process for obtaining witnesses in his favor and to have the assistance of counsel in his defense.

Sec. 7. DUE PROCESS; PROSECUTIONS; DOUBLE JEOPARDY; SELF-INCRIMINATION; BAIL; HABEAS CORPUS. No person shall be held to answer for a criminal offense without due process of law, and no person shall be put twice in jeopardy of punishment for the same offense, nor be compelled in any criminal case to be a witness against himself, nor be deprived of life, liberty or property without due process of law. All persons before conviction shall be bailable by sufficient sureties, except for capital offenses when the proof is evident or the presumption great. The privilege of the writ of habeas corpus shall not be suspended unless the public safety requires it in case of rebellion or invasion.

Sec. 8. REDRESS OF INJURIES OR WRONGS. Every person is entitled to a certain remedy in the laws for all injuries or wrongs which he may receive to his person, property or character, and to obtain justice freely and without purchase, completely and without denial, promptly and without delay, conformable to the laws.

Sec. 9. TREASON DEFINED. Treason against the state consists only in levying war against the state, or in adhering to its enemies, giving them aid and comfort. No person shall be convicted of treason unless on the testimony of two witnesses to the same overt act or on confession in open court.

Sec. 10. UNREASONABLE SEARCHES AND SEIZURES PROHIBITED. The right of the people to be secure in their persons, houses, papers, and effects against unreasonable searches and seizures shall not be violated; and no warrant shall issue but upon probable cause, supported by oath or affirmation, and particularly describing the place to be searched and the person or things to be seized.

Sec. 11. ATTAINDERS, EX POST FACTO LAWS AND LAWS IMPAIRING CONTRACTS PROHIBITED. No bill of attainder, ex post facto law, or any law impairing the obligation of contracts shall be passed, and no conviction shall work corruption of blood or forfeiture of estate.

Sec. 12. IMPRISONMENT FOR DEBT; PROPERTY EXEMPTION. No person shall be imprisoned for debt in this state, but this shall not prevent the legislature from providing for imprisonment, or holding to bail, persons charged with fraud in contracting said debt. A reasonable amount of property shall be exempt from seizure or sale for the payment of any debt or liability. The amount of such exemption shall be determined by law. Provided, however, that all property so exempted shall be liable to seizure and sale for any debts incurred to any person for work done or materials furnished in the construction, repair or improvement of the same, and provided further, that such liability to seizure and sale shall also extend to all real property for any debt to any laborer or servant for labor or service performed.

Sec. 13. **PRIVATE PROPERTY FOR PUBLIC USE.** Private property shall not be taken, destroyed or damaged for public use without just compensation therefor, first paid or secured.

Sec. 14. **MILITARY POWER SUBORDINATE.** The military shall be subordinate to the civil power and no standing army shall be maintained in this state in times of peace.

Sec. 15. **LANDS ALLODIAL; VOID AGRICULTURAL LEASES.** All lands within the state are allodial and feudal tenures of every description with all their incidents are prohibited. Leases and grants of agricultural lands for a longer period than 21 years reserving rent or service of any kind shall be void.

Sec. 16. **FREEDOM OF CONSCIENCE; NO PREFERENCE TO BE GIVEN TO ANY RELIGIOUS ESTABLISHMENT OR MODE OF WORSHIP.** The enumeration of rights in this constitution shall not deny or impair others retained by and inherent in the people. The right of every man to worship God according to the dictates of his own conscience shall never be infringed; nor shall any man be compelled to attend, erect or support any place of worship, or to maintain any religious or ecclesiastical ministry, against his consent; nor shall any control of or interference with the rights of conscience be permitted, or any preference be given by law to any religious establishment or mode of worship; but the liberty of conscience hereby secured shall not be so construed as to excuse acts of licentiousness or justify practices inconsistent with the peace or safety of the state, nor shall any money be drawn from the treasury for the benefit of any religious societies or religious or theological seminaries.

Sec. 17. RELIGIOUS TESTS AND PROPERTY QUALIFICA-TIONS PROHIBITED. No religious test or amount of property shall be required as a qualification for any office of public trust in the state. No religious test or amount of property shall be required as a qualification of any voter at any election in this state; nor shall any person be rendered incompetent to give evidence in any court of law or equity in consequence of his opinion upon the subject of religion.

ARTICLE II—NAME AND BOUNDARIES

Section 1. NAME AND BOUNDARIES; ACCEPTANCE OF ORGANIC ACT. This state shall be called the state of_____and shall consist of and have jurisdiction over the territory embraced in [ ]. The propositions contained in that act are hereby accepted, ratified and confirmed, and remain irrevocable without the consent of the United States.

Sec. 2. JURISDICTION ON BOUNDARY WATERS. The state has concurrent jurisdiction on all other rivers and waters forming a common boundary with any other state or states. Navigable waters leading into the same, shall be common highways and forever free to citizens of the United States without any tax, duty, impost or toll therefor.

ARTICLE III—STRUCTURE AND FUNCTIONS OF GOVERNMENT

The people of this State, reserving to themselves the right "to institute new government…as to them shall seem most likely to effect their safety and happiness," vest their sovereign authority in the Legislature of this State, which shall be deemed to consist of: the Governor, the College of Legates, and the House of Representatives.

SECTION 1. THE GOVERNOR

Subsec. 1. AUTHORITY The authority of the head of state shall be vested in the office of the Governor.

Subsec 2. ELECTION The Governor shall be chosen in the following manner:

The College of Legates shall sit in Convention on the second Monday in January following the adoption of this Constitution, and the second Monday of January every fifth year following, for the sole purpose of proposing to the people candidates for the Governorship.

The College shall nominate at least two but no more than five candidates for the Governorship. The College shall determine by its own rules how nominations shall be accomplished.

On the first Sunday in February following nominations by the College, the people shall elect one of the persons nominated as Governor of the State. The candidate receiving the most votes shall be declared elected.

Subsec. 3. OATH OF OFFICE. The person elected Governor shall be sworn into office on the first Monday in March following the election. Upon inauguration the Governor-elect shall make the following oath or affirmation, and thereupon attain the office:

"I, N., do solemnly swear (or affirm) that I will faithfully execute the office of Governor of this State, and will to the best of my Ability, preserve, protect, and defend the Constitution of this State, and the Constitution of the United States."

Subsec. 4. QUALIFICATIONS The following shall be the qualifications for the Governorship:

Attainment of the age of 35 years;

Registration as a voter in this State;

Not being registered as a member of a political party;

Not being a member or a former member of the committee of any political party;

Not being a lobbyist, defined by common usage of the term or by an Act of the Legislature;

Not having contributed more than $500 to any political candidate in the ten years before the nomination;

Not currently holding any office of profit or trust under the United States, or any of them, or any State subdivision, except as provided below.

Subsec. 5. REPRESENTATIVES AND LEGATES ELIGIBLE FOR GOVERNORSHIP Former members of the House of Representatives or of the College of Legates shall be eligible for nomination for the Governorship, but the provisions of subsections a., b., e., and f., of Section 4 above shall still apply.

Subsec. 6. RENOMINATION The incumbent Governor shall be eligible for re-nomination, but only once.

Subsec. 7. CAMPAIGN EXPENSE LIMITS Campaign expenses for the Governorship shall be limited to the value of $200,000 per candidate as it existed at the time of the adoption of this Constitution, unless provided for otherwise by Act of the Legislature.

Subsec. 8. REMOVAL OF THE GOVERNOR In case of the Removal of the Governor from Office, or of the Governor's Death, Resignation, or Inability to discharge the Powers and

Duties of his Office, the same shall devolve upon the Chancellor of the College of Legates, who shall take the oath of the Governorship, become Governor, and complete the balance of the incumbent term; any further provision on this question shall be regulated by Act of the Legislature.

Subsec. 9. COMPENSATION OF THE GOVERNOR The Governor shall receive at stated Times receive for his Services, a Compensation, which shall be neither increased nor diminished during the Period for which he shall be elected, and he shall not receive within that period any other Emolument from the United States, or any of them.

Subsec. 10. DUTIES OF THE GOVERNOR.

The Governor shall be Commander-in-Chief of the Armed Forces of this State, but will act in this capacity only on the advice of the appropriate Minister of State;

He may require the Opinion, in writing, of the principal Officer in each of the executive Departments, upon any Subject relating to the Duties of their respective Offices;

He shall have the Power, subject to the advice of the appropriate Minister of State, to grant Reprieves and Pardons for Offenses against the United States, except in cases of Impeachment;

He shall appoint, upon the advice of the appropriate Minister of State, all other Officers of the United States, whose Appointments are not herein otherwise provided for: but the Legislature may by Law vest the appointment of such inferior Officers, as they think proper, in the Courts of Law, or in the Heads of Departments.

He shall at the beginning of each session of the Legislature present an Address on the State of the State, in which Address the Governor, on the advice of the Administration, shall recommend to their consideration such measures as he considers necessary and expedient, and give notice of the Estimates for the Public Service to be laid before the House; to which Address the House of Representatives shall debate and vote a Reply.

He may, on extraordinary occasions, convene the College of Legates or the House of Representatives, or both.

He shall dissolve the House of Representatives and order new elections to the House on the advice of the Premier, though he may in his absolute discretion, refuse to dissolve the House on the advice of a Premier who has ceased to retain the support of a majority of the House of Representatives.

He shall take care that the Laws shall be faithfully executed, and shall Commission all the Officers of this State.

Subsec. 11. GOVERNOR'S ASSENT. A Bill passed by the House of Representatives shall become law when the Governor assents to it, upon the advice of the Premier, and signs it in token of such assent.

Subsec 12. ADVICE OF THE ADMINISTRATION The powers conferred upon the President shall be exercised by him only upon the advice of the Administration.

Section 2. THE COLLEGE OF LEGATES

Subsec. 1. PURPOSE. The non-partisan supervision of the Government on behalf of the people shall be vested in the College of Legates.

Subsec. 2. MEMBERSHIP. The College shall consist of one Legate from each of the counties of this state.

Subsec. 3. NOMINATION. On the first Monday in January following the adoption of this Constitution, and every third year thereafter, the legislative authority of each county shall sit in their respective county seats for the purpose of nominating candidates for the Legateship of that county.

The Legislature shall establish standard rules for nominations to the Legateship.

The legislative authority in each county shall nominate at least three but no more than five candidates for the Legateship.

Subsec. 4. ELECTION. On the second Sunday following the nomination, the people shall vote for their Legates. The candidate receiving the most votes shall be elected Legate.

Subsec. 5. OATH OF OFFICE. On the second Monday following the election, the Legates shall proceed to their respective county seat, where they shall subscribe the following oath from the Executive Authority thereof:

"I, N., do solemnly swear (or affirm) that I will faithfully execute the high office of Legate, and will to the best of my ability, preserve, protect, and defend the Constitution of this States, and the Constitution of the United States."

Subsec. 6. ASSEMBLY OF LEGATES. On the Monday following taking their oaths, the Legates shall assemble in the State Capitol building, under the temporary presidency of a Delegate of the Governor, and shall proceed immediately to the election of one of their number as Chancellor of the College and another as Vice-Chancellor.

Subsec. 7. COINCIDENCE OF ELECTIONS. When a year occurs that the election of the Governor and the election of Legates coincide, the election of Legates shall begin on the first Monday of March, and proceed in the same fashion as if it took place on the first Monday in January.

Subsec. 8. COMPENSATION OF LEGATES. The Legates shall receive for their Services a Compensation, to be paid out of the State Treasury, which compensation shall not be increased nor decreased during their terms of office. The Legates shall not receive any other compensation for anything else, other than income from previous or current investments, during their term of office.

Subsec 9. QUALIFICATIONS OF LEGATES. Candidates for the College of Legates shall have the following qualifications:

They shall have attained to the full age of Thirty years;

They shall be registered voters and residents of the county they represent;

They shall not be registered members of any political party, as defined by the laws this state or, if political affiliation is not declared at registration, shall not be members of the committee of any political party;

They shall not be lobbyists as defined by the common meaning of the word or by applicable law;

They shall not have made a contribution of more than $100 to any one political candidate, nor more than $1000 altogether, in the five years prior to their election;

They shall currently hold no office of profit or trust of the United States, or any of them, or their subdivisions.

Subsec. 10. RE-ELECTION. Incumbent Legates are eligible for re-election.

Subsec. 11. CAMPAIGN EXPENSES. Campaign expenses for candidates to the College of Legates shall not exceed the value of $5,000 (per candidate) as it existed at the adoption of this Constitution.

Subsec. 12. NO CONSIDERATION OF LEGISLATION. No bill, order, vote, or resolution of the House of Representatives shall be in order for consideration by the College of Legates.

Subsec. 13. AUTHORITY. The Authority of the College of Legates shall extend to:

The nomination of candidates for the Governor, in accordance with the provisions of this Constitution;

The appointment of a Committee of Legates as a Boundary Commission for seats in the House of Representatives;

The appointment of an Auditor-General, who shall head the accounting office of the Government as provided by law;

The appointment of a Statistician-General, who shall be in charge of the statistical functions of the Government, as provided by law;

The appointment of the Librarian of the Legislature;

The appointment of the Attorney-General as chief legal adviser to the Government;

The appointment of the Procurator-General of the State, and the chief prosecutors of the judicial districts of the State;

The appointment of the Secretary of State as the chief clerk of the Government;

The examination into complaints from citizens of this State of wrongdoing by officials of this State, and the exposure and public humiliation of any public official committing any act of wrongdoing against any private person, for which the College shall have the power of subpoena, and if criminal wrongdoing shall be found, shall refer the matter for prosection to the appropriate authorities;

The authority to recommend to the House of Representatives a scale of compensation and benefits for the Governor, the Representatives, the Premier, the Ministers of State, the Leader of the Opposition, the Shadow Ministers, the Whips and the other Leaders of Caucus—the House of Representatives may accept or reject their recommendation but may not alter it on its own motion;

The authority to pass resolutions expressing the sense of the College on any matter, these resolutions being understood to have no force of law; Any authority delegated to it by Act of the Legislature, which may be withdrawn at any time by another Act of the Legislature.

Subsec. 14. ESTABLISHMENT OF RULES. The College shall determine the Rules of its Proceedings, punish Members for disorderly conduct, and, with the concurrence of two-thirds of the whole College, expel a Member and request that the legislative authority of the county concerned immediately appoint a successor to fill out the term of the expelled Legate.

Subsec. 15. VERBATIM JOURNAL. The College shall keep a verbatim Journal of its proceedings and publish it from time to time, excepting such parts as may in its Judgement require Secrecy, and the Yeas and Nays of the Legates on any question, on the request of one-fifth of the members present, shall be entered in the Journal.

Section 3. THE HOUSE OF REPRESENTATIVES

Subsec. 1. AUTHORITY. All legislative powers herein granted shall be vested in the House of Representatives.

Subsec. 2 MEMBERSHIP

The House of Representatives shall consist of Members chosen by the people of this State.

The House shall consist between of 130 and 150 Members, with one Representative returned from each district.

A committee of the College of Legates shall propose a plan after each decennial census for the re-apportion-ment of the House of Representatives. The House shall approve or disapprove of the plan as it sees fit, but may not alter the plan on its own motion.

The apportionment plan shall divide this State into as many districts as there are Representatives. The districts shall consist of compact and contiguous territory. All districts shall be so nearly equal in population that the population of the smallest does not vary from the pop-ulation of the largest by more than five per cent.

Subsec. 3. QUALIFICATIONS.

No person shall be a representative who shall not have attained to the age of twenty-five years, be a citizen of the United States, and have been three years a resident of this State.

Campaign expenses for candidates to the House of Representatives shall not exceed the value of $10,000 (per candidate) as it exists at the time of the adoption of this Constitution.

Subsec. 4. VACANCIES. When vacancies occur in the House, the Speaker shall promptly issue writs of election to fill such vacancies.

Subsec. 5. SUMMONS FOR SESSION. The Governor shall from Time to Time, by instrument under the Great Seal of this State, summon and call together the House of Representatives.

Subsec. 6. LEGATES DISQUALIFIED. A member of the College of Legates shall not be capable of being elected or of sitting or voting as a member of the House of Representatives.

Subsec. 7. ELECTION OF SPEAKER. The House of Representatives shall, at its first meeting after any general election of its members, and immediately after any vacancy occurs in the office of Speaker, choose one of its members as Speaker, and every such choice shall be effective on being confirmed by the Governor.

Subsec. 8. PRESIDENCY OF SPEAKER. The Speaker shall preside at all sittings of the House, and the House shall provide, by its own rules, for the case of the absence of the Speaker for more than forty-eight hours.

Subsec. 9. OATH OF REPRESENTATIVES. A Representative shall not be permitted to sit or vote in the House until he has sworn or affirmed the following oath before the Governor or a person authorized by him to administer the oath:

"I, N., do solemnly swear (or affirm) that I shall faithfully execute the office of Representative, and will to the best of my ability, preserve, protect, and defend the

Constitution of this State, and the Constitution of the United States."

Subsec. 10. TERM OF HOUSE. Every House of Representatives shall continue for Four Years from the day of the Return of the Writs for choosing the House, and no longer, subject to being sooner dissolved by the Governor.

Subsec. 11. RE-ORGANIZATION OF HOUSE. After any general election, the House shall meet no later than three weeks after the day fixed for the Return of the Writs of that election.

Subsec. 12. MESSAGE OF THE GOVERNOR. It shall not be lawful for the House to adopt or pass any Vote, Resolution, Address, or Bill for Appropriation of any Part of the Public Revenue, or of any Tax or Impost, to any purpose that has not been recommended by Message of the President in the Session in which such Vote, Resolution, Address, or Bill for Appropriation is proposed.

Subsec. 13. LIMITATION OF APPROPRIATION. It shall not be lawful for the House of Representatives, except by or under an Act of the House of Representatives:

- to levy a tax;
- to raise a loan or receive any money as a loan from any person;
- or to spend any public money.

Subsec. 14. JUDGE OF ELECTIONS; QUORUM. The House shall be the Judge of the Elections, Returns, and Qualifications of its Members, and a Majority shall constitute a Quorum to do Business; but a smaller Number may adjourn from day to day and may be authorized to compel the attendance of absent Members, in such manner and under such Penalties as the House may provide.

Subsec. 15. RULES. The House may determine the Rules of its Proceedings, punish Members for disorderly Behavior, and, with the concurrence of two-thirds, expel a Member.

Subsec. 16. VERBATIM JOURNAL. The House shall keep a verbatim Journal of its proceedings, and shall from time to time publish it, excepting such parts as may in its judgement require Secrecy; and the Yeas and Nays of the Members of the House on any question shall, at the desire of one-fifth of those present, be entered on the Journal.

Subsec. 17. PRIVILEGE FROM ARREST. Representatives and Legates shall in all Cases, except Treason, Felony, and Breach of the Peace, be privileged from Arrest during their attendance at the Session of their respective Houses, and in going to and returning from the same; and for any speech or debate in either House, they shall not be questioned in any other place.

Subsec. 18. FORM OF LAWS. No law shall be passed except by bill, and no bill except bills for appropriations and bills for the codification, rearrangement, or revision of existing laws, shall have more than one subject.

Subsec. 19. PASSAGE OF LAWS. No bill shall become a law unless it has been printed and in the designated mailboxes of the members in final form at least three days prior to final passage, and the majority of all the members has assented to it. The yeas and nays on final passage shall be entered into the journal and published.

Subsec. 20. COMMITTEES. The House of Representatives may establish such committees it shall deem necessary for the conduct of its business. These committees shall be governed by Rules established by the House.

Subsec 21. ANNUAL MEETINGS. The House shall assemble at least once in every year, and such meeting shall begin at noon on the second Monday of January, unless they shall by law appoint a different day.

Section 4. THE ADMINISTRATION

Subsec. 1. EXECUTIVE POWERS. The executive Powers of the Legislature shall be governed by the Administration.

Subsec. 2. MEMBERSHIP. The Administration shall consist of the Premier and such other Ministers of State as the Governor, on the advice of the Premier, shall appoint.

Subsec. 3. TITLE. The head of the Administration shall be called, and in this Constitution is referred to as the Premier.

Subsec. 4 SEALS OF OFFICE

The Governor shall grant the Seals of the Office of Premier to that Member of the House of Representatives who commands the Majority of the House.

The Governor shall grant the Seal of Office of a Ministry of State to any Representative whom the Premier designates; the Governor shall withdraw the seals of a minister on the advice of the Premier.

Subsec. 5. MINISTERIAL QUALIFICATION. No Person shall be granted the Seals of Office of Premier or Minister of State unless he is also a Member of the House of Representatives.

Subsec. 6. COLLECTIVE RESPONSIBILITY. The Administration shall be collectively responsible for the Departments of State.

Subsec. 7. ESTIMATES. The Administration each year shall prepare Estimates of the Receipts and Expenditures of the Public Service, and shall lay these Estimates for consideration by the House.

Subsec. 8. RESIGNATION

The Premier may resign at any time by surrendering the Seals of Office to the Governor.

Any member of the Administration may resign by surrendering the Seals of Office to the Premier for submission to the Governor

The Governor shall accept the resignation of a member of the Adminstration, other than the Premier, if so advised by the Premier.

The Members of the Adminsitration in office at the date of the dissolution of the House shall continue to hold office until their successors are appointed.

Subsec. 9. NO CONFIDENCE IN ADMINISTRATION. It shall be in order at any time for the Leader of the Official Opposition to lay before the House the motion, "This House has no confidence in the present Administration," and if the motion shall pass, the Administration shall resign, and the Premier shall request that the Governor dissolve the House and issue writs for a new election, as provided in this Constitution.

Subsec. 10. MINISTERS SUBJECT TO QUESTIONING. During each day's sitting of the House, at least one hour shall be devoted to questioning Ministers of State on the performance of their duties; at least 40 minutes a week shall be reserved for questioning the Premier or his designated representative.

ARTICLE IV—THE JUDICIARY

Section 1. JUDICIAL POWER. The judicial power of the state is vested in a supreme court, a court of appeals, if established by the legislature, a district court and such other courts, judicial officers and commissioners with jurisdiction inferior to the district court as the legislature may establish.

Sec. 2. SUPREME COURT. The supreme court consists of one chief judge and not less than six nor more than eight associate judges as the legislature may establish. It shall have original jurisdiction in such remedial cases as are prescribed by law, and appellate jurisdiction in all cases, but there shall be no trial by jury in the supreme court. The legislature may establish a court of appeals and provide by law for the number of its judges, who shall not be judges of any other court, and its organization and for the review of its decisions by the supreme court. The court of appeals shall have appellate jurisdiction over all courts, except the supreme court, and other appellate jurisdiction as prescribed by law. As provided by law judges of the court of appeals or of the district court may be assigned temporarily to act as judges of the supreme court upon its request and judges of the district court may be assigned temporarily by the supreme court to act as judges of the court of appeals.

The supreme court shall appoint to serve at its pleasure a clerk, a reporter, a state law librarian and other necessary employees.

Sec. 3. JURISDICTION OF DISTRICT COURT. The district court has original jurisdiction in all civil and criminal cases and shall have appellate jurisdiction as prescribed by law.

Sec. 4. JUDICIAL DISTRICTS; DISTRICT JUDGES. The number and boundaries of judicial districts shall be established in the manner provided by law but the office of a district judge shall not be abolished during his term. There shall be two or more district judges in each district. Each judge of the district court in any district shall be a resident of that district at the time of his selection and during his continuance in office.

Sec. 5. QUALIFICATIONS; COMPENSATION. Judges of the supreme court, the court of appeals and the district court shall be learned in the law. The qualifications of all other judges and judicial officers shall be prescribed by law. The compensation of all judges shall be prescribed by the legislature and shall not be diminished during their term of office.

Sec. 6. HOLDING OTHER OFFICE. A judge of the supreme court, the court of appeals or the district court shall not hold any office under the United States except a commission in a reserve component of the military forces of the United States and shall not hold any other office under this state. His term of office shall terminate at the time he files as a candidate for an elective office of the United States or for a nonjudicial office of this state.

Sec. 7. TERM OF OFFICE; ELECTION. The term of office of all judges shall be six years and until their successors are qualified. They shall be elected by the voters from the area which they are to serve in the manner provided by law.

Sec. 8. VACANCY. Whenever there is a vacancy in the office of judge the governor shall appoint in the manner provided by law a qualified person to fill the vacancy until a successor is elected and qualified. The successor shall be elected for a six year term at the next general election occurring more than one year after the appointment.

Sec. 9. RETIREMENT, REMOVAL AND DISCIPLINE. The legislature may provide by law for retirement of all judges and for the extension of the term of any judge who becomes eligible for retirement within three years after expiration of the term for which he is selected. The legislature may also provide for the retirement, removal or other discipline of any judge who is disabled, incompetent or guilty of conduct prejudicial to the administration of justice.

Sec. 10. RETIRED JUDGES. As provided by law a retired judge may be assigned to hear and decide any cause over which the court to which he is assigned has jurisdiction.

Sec. 11. PROBATE JURISDICTION. Original jurisdiction in law and equity for the administration of the estates of deceased persons and all guardianship and incompetency proceedings, including jurisdiction over the administration of trust estates and for the determination of taxes contingent upon death, shall be provided by law.

Sec. 12. ABOLITION OF PROBATE COURT; STATUS OF JUDGES. If the probate court is abolished by law, judges of that court who are learned in the law shall become judges of the court that assumes jurisdiction of matters described in section 11.

Sec. 13. DISTRICT COURT CLERKS. There shall be in each county one clerk of the district court whose qualifications, duties and compensation shall be prescribed by law. He shall serve at the pleasure of a majority of the judges of the district court in each district.

ARTICLE V—ELECTIVE FRANCHISE

Section 1. ELIGIBILITY; PLACE OF VOTING; INELIGIBLE PERSONS. Every person 18 years of age or more who has been a citizen of the United States for three months and who has resided in the precinct for 30 days next preceding an election shall be entitled to vote in that precinct. The place of voting by one otherwise qualified who has changed his residence within 30 days preceding the election shall be prescribed by law.

The following persons shall not be entitled or permitted to vote at any election in this state:

- A person not meeting the above requirements;

- A person who has been convicted of treason or felony, unless restored to civil rights;

- A person under guardianship, or a person who is insane or not mentally competent.

Sec. 2. RESIDENCE. For the purpose of voting no person loses residence solely by reason of his absence while employed in the service of the United States; nor while engaged upon the waters of this state or of the United States; nor while a student in any institution of learning; nor while kept at any almshouse or asylum; nor while confined in any public prison. No soldier, seaman or marine in the army or navy of the United States is a resident of this state solely in consequence of being stationed within the state.

Sec. 3. UNIFORM OATH AT ELECTIONS. The legislature shall provide for a uniform oath or affirmation to be administered at elections and no person shall be compelled to take any other or different form of oath to entitle him to vote.

Sec. 4. CIVIL PROCESS SUSPENDED ON ELECTION DAY. During the day on which an election is held no person shall be arrested by virtue of any civil process.

Sec. 5. ELECTIONS BY BALLOT. All elections shall be by ballot except for such town officers as may be directed by law to be otherwise chosen.

Sec. 6. ELIGIBILITY TO HOLD OFFICE. Every person who by the provisions of this article is entitled to vote at any election and is 21 years of age is eligible for any office elective by the people in the district wherein he has resided 30 days previous to the election, except as otherwise provided in this constitution, or the constitution and law of the United States.

Sec. 7. OFFICIAL YEAR OF STATE. The official year for the state of Minnesota commences on the first Monday in January in each year.

Sec. 8. ELECTION RETURNS TO REGISTRAR OF ELECTIONS; BOARD OF CANVASSERS. The returns of every election for officeholders elected statewide shall be made to the registrar of elections who shall call to his assistance two or more of the judges of the supreme court and two disinterested judges of the district courts. They shall constitute a board of canvassers to canvass the returns and declare the result within three days after the canvass.

Sec. 9. CAMPAIGN SPENDING LIMITS. The amount that may be spent by candidates for constitutional and legislative offices, other than otherwise provided in this constitution, to campaign for nomination or election shall be limited by law. The legislature shall provide by law for disclosure of contributions and expenditures made to support or oppose candidates for state elective offices.

ARTICLE VI—IMPEACHMENT AND REMOVAL FROM OFFICE

Section 1. IMPEACHMENT POWERS. The House of Representatives has the sole power of impeachment through a concurrence of a majority of all its members. All impeachments shall be tried by the College of Legates. When sitting for that purpose, the Legates shall be upon oath or affirmation to do justice according to law and evidence. No person shall be convicted without the concurrence of two-thirds of the Legates present.

Sec. 2. OFFICERS SUBJECT TO IMPEACHMENT; GROUNDS; JUDGMENT. The governor, the judges of the supreme court, court of appeals and district courts may be impeached for corrupt conduct in office or for crimes and misdemeanors; but judgment shall not extend further than to removal from office and disqualification to hold and enjoy any office of honor, trust or profit in this state. The party convicted shall also be subject to indictment, trial, judgment and punishment according to law.

Sec. 3. SUSPENSION. No officer shall exercise the duties of his office after he has been impeached and before his acquittal.

Sec. 4. SERVICE OF IMPEACHMENT PAPERS. No person shall be tried on impeachment before he has been served with a copy thereof at least 20 days previous to the day set for trial.

Sec. 5. REMOVAL OF INFERIOR OFFICERS. The legislature of this state may provide for the removal of inferior officers for malfeasance or nonfeasance in the performance of their duties.

ARTICLE VII—AMENDMENTS TO THE CONSTITUTION

Section 1. AMENDMENTS; RATIFICATION. If a majority of all the electors voting at the election vote to ratify an amendment, it becomes a part of this constitution. If two or more amendments are submitted at the same time, voters shall vote for or against each separately.

Sec. 2. CONSTITUTIONAL CONVENTION. If a majority of all the electors voting at the election vote for a convention, the legislature at its next session, shall provide by law for calling the convention. The convention shall consist of as many delegates as there are members of the house of representatives. Delegates shall be chosen in the same manner as members of the house of representatives and shall meet within three months after their election.

Sec. 3. SUBMISSION TO PEOPLE OF CONSTITUTION DRAFTED AT CONVENTION. A convention called to revise this constitution shall submit any revision to the people for approval or rejection at the next general election held not less than 90 days after submission of the revision. If three-fifths of all the electors voting on the question vote to ratify the revision, it becomes a new constitution of this state.

ARTICLE VIII—TAXATION

Section 1. POWER OF TAXATION; EXEMPTIONS; LEGISLATIVE POWERS. The power of taxation shall never be surrendered, suspended or contracted away. Taxes shall be uniform upon the same class of subjects and shall be levied and collected for public purposes, but public burying grounds, public school houses, public hospitals, academies, colleges, universities, all seminaries of learning, all churches, church property, houses of worship, institutions of purely public charity, and public property used exclusively for any public purpose, shall be exempt from taxation except as provided in this section. There may be exempted from taxation personal property not exceeding in value $200 for each household, individual or head of a family, and household goods and farm machinery as the legislature determines. The legislature may authorize municipal corporations to levy and collect assessments for local improvements upon property benefited thereby without regard to cash valuation. The legislature by law may define or limit the property exempt under this section other than churches, houses of worship, and property solely used for educational purposes by academies, colleges, universities and seminaries of learning.

Sec. 2. FORESTATION. To encourage and promote forestation and reforestation of lands whether owned by private persons or the public, laws may be enacted fixing in advance a definite and limited annual tax on the lands for a term of years and imposing a yield tax on the timber and other forest products at or after the end of the term.

Sec. 3. OCCUPATION TAX; ORES. Every person engaged in the business of mining or producing iron ore or other ores in this state shall pay to the state an occupation tax on the valuation of all ores mined or produced, which tax shall be in addition to all other taxes provided by law. The tax is due on the first day of May in the calendar year next following the mining or producing. The valuation of ore for the purpose of determining the amount of tax shall be ascertained as provided by law.

Sec. 4. MOTOR FUEL TAXATION. The state may levy an excise tax upon any means or substance for propelling aircraft or for propelling or operating motor or other vehicles or other equipment used for airport purposes and not used on the public highways of this state.

Sec. 5. AIRCRAFT. The legislature may tax aircraft using the air space overlying the state on a more onerous basis than other personal property. Any such tax on aircraft shall be in lieu of all other taxes. The legislature may impose the tax on aircraft of companies paying taxes under any gross earnings system of taxation notwithstanding that earnings from the aircraft are included in the earnings on which gross earnings taxes are computed. The law may exempt from taxation aircraft owned by a nonresident of the state temporarily using the air space overlying the state.

Sec. 6. PARIMUTUEL BETTING. The legislature may authorize on-track parimutuel betting on horse racing in a manner prescribed by law.

ARTICLE IX—APPROPRIATIONS AND FINANCES

Section 1. MONEY PAID FROM STATE TREASURY. No money shall be paid out of the treasury of this state except in pursuance of an appropriation by law.

Sec. 2. CREDIT OF THE STATE LIMITED. The credit of the state shall not be given or lent in aid of any individual, association or corporation except as hereinafter provided.

Sec. 3. INTERNAL IMPROVEMENTS PROHIBITED; EXCEPTIONS. The state shall not be a party in carrying on works of internal improvements except as authorized by this constitution. If grants have been made to the state especially dedicated to specific purposes, the state shall devote the proceeds of the grants to those purposes and may pledge or appropriate the revenues derived from the works in aid of their completion.

Sec. 4. POWER TO CONTRACT PUBLIC DEBT; PUBLIC DEBT DEFINED. The state may contract public debts for which its full faith, credit and taxing powers may be pledged at the times and in the manner authorized by law, but only for the purposes and subject to the conditions stated in section 5. Public debt includes any obligation payable directly in whole or in part from a tax of state wide application on any class of property, income, transaction or privilege, but does not include any obligation which is payable from revenues other than taxes.

WORKS OF INTERNAL IMPROVEMENT; PURPOSES. Public debt may be contracted and works of internal improvements carried on for the following purposes:

to acquire and to better public land and buildings and other public improvements of a capital nature and to provide money to be appropriated or loaned to any agency or political subdivision of the state for such purposes if the law authorizing the debt is adopted by the vote of at least three-fifths of the members of each house of the legislature;

to repel invasion or suppress insurrection;

to borrow temporarily as authorized in section 6;

to refund outstanding bonds of the state or any of its agencies whether or not the full faith and credit of the state has been pledged for the payment of the bonds;

to establish and maintain highways subject to the limitations of article XIV;

to promote forestation and prevent and abate forest fires, including the compulsory clearing and improving of wild lands whether public or private;

to construct, improve and operate airports and other air navigation facilities;

to develop the state's agricultural resources by extending credit on real estate security in the manner and on the terms and conditions prescribed by law;

to improve and rehabilitate railroad rights-of-way and other rail facilities whether public or private, provided that bonds issued and unpaid shall not at any time exceed $200,000,000 par value; and as otherwise authorized in this constitution.

As authorized by law political subdivisions may engage in the works permitted by (f), (g), and (i) and contract debt therefor.

Sec. 6. CERTIFICATES OF INDEBTEDNESS. As authorized by law certificates of indebtedness may be issued during a biennium, commencing on July 1 in each odd-numbered year and ending on and including June 30 in the next odd-numbered year, in anticipation of the collection of taxes levied for and other revenues appropriated to any fund of the state for expenditure during that biennium.

No certificates shall be issued in an amount which with interest thereon to maturity, added to the then outstanding certificates against a fund and interest thereon to maturity, will exceed the then unexpended balance of all money which will be credited to that fund during the biennium under existing laws.

The maturities of certificates may be extended by refunding to a date not later than December 1 of the first full calendar year following the biennium in which the certificates were issued. If money on hand in any fund is not sufficient to pay all non-refunding certificates of indebtedness issued on a fund during any biennium and all certificates refunding the same, plus interest thereon, which are outstanding on December 1 immediately following the close of the biennium, the state auditor shall levy upon all taxable property in the state a tax collectible in the ensuing year sufficient to pay the same on or before December 1 of the ensuing year with interest to the date or dates of payment.

Sec. 7. BONDS. Public debt other than certificates of indebtedness authorized in section 6 shall be evidenced by the issuance of bonds of the state. All bonds issued under the provisions of this section shall mature not more than 20 years from their respective dates of issue and each law authorizing the issuance of bonds shall distinctly specify the purposes thereof and the maximum amount of the proceeds authorized to be expended for each purpose. A separate and special state bond fund shall be maintained on the official books and records.

When the full faith and credit of the state has been pledged for the payment of bonds, the state auditor shall levy each year on all taxable property within the state a tax sufficient with the balance then on hand in the fund to pay all principal and interest on bonds issued under this section due and to become due within the ensuing year and to and including July 1 in the second ensuing year. The legislature by law may appropriate funds from any source to the state bond fund. The amount of money actually received and on hand pursuant to appropriations prior to the levy of the tax in any year shall be used to reduce the amount of tax otherwise required to be levied.

Sec. 8. PERMANENT SCHOOL FUND; SOURCE; INVEST-MENT; BOARD OF INVESTMENT. The permanent school fund of the state consists of the proceeds of lands granted by the United States for the use of schools within each township, the proceeds derived from swamp lands granted to the state, all cash and investments credited to the permanent school fund and to the swamp land fund, and all cash and investments credited to the internal improvement land fund and the lands therein.

No portion of these lands shall be sold otherwise than at public sale, and in the manner provided by law. All funds arising from the sale or other disposition of the lands, or income accruing in any way before the sale or disposition thereof, shall be credited to the permanent school fund.

Within limitations prescribed by law, the fund shall be invested to secure the maximum return consistent with the maintenance of the perpetuity of the fund. The principal of the permanent school fund shall be perpetual and inviolate forever. This does not prevent the sale of investments at less than the cost to the fund; however, all losses not offset by gains shall be repaid to the fund from the interest and dividends earned thereafter. The net interest and dividends arising from the fund shall be distributed to the different school districts of the state in a manner prescribed by law.

A board of investment consisting of the Governor, the Auditor-General, and the attorney general is constituted for the purpose of administering and directing the investment of all state funds. The board shall not permit state funds to be used for the underwriting or direct purchase of municipal securities from the issuer or the issuer's agent.

Sec. 9. INVESTMENT OF PERMANENT UNIVERSITY FUND; RESTRICTIONS. The permanent university fund of this state may be lent to or invested in the bonds of any county, school district, city or town of this state and in first mortgage loans secured upon improved and cultivated farm lands of this state, but no such investment or loan shall be made until approved by the board of investment; nor shall a loan or investment be made when the bonds to be issued or purchased would make the entire bonded indebtedness exceed 15 percent of the assessed valuation of the taxable property of the county, school district, city or town issuing the bonds; nor shall any farm loan or investment be made when the investment or loan would exceed 30 percent of the actual cash value of the farm land mortgaged to secure the investment; nor shall investments or loans be made at a lower rate of interest than two percent per annum nor for a shorter period than one year nor for a longer period than 30 years.

Sec. 10. EXCHANGE OF PUBLIC LANDS; RESERVATION OF RIGHTS. As the legislature may provide, any of the public lands of the state, including lands held in trust for any purpose, may be exchanged for any publicly or privately held lands with the unanimous approval of the Governor, the Attorney General and the Auditor-General. Lands so acquired shall be subject to the trust, if any, to which the lands exchanged therefor were subject. The state shall reserve all mineral and water power rights in lands transferred by the state.

Sec. 11. TIMBER LANDS SET APART AS STATE FORESTS; DISPOSITION OF REVENUE. School and other public lands of the state better adapted for the production of timber than for agriculture may be set apart as state school forests, or other state forests as the legislature may provide. The legislature may also provide for their management on forestry principles. The net revenue therefrom shall be used for the purposes for which the lands were granted to the state.

Sec. 12. COUNTY, TOWNSHIP OR MUNICIPAL AID TO RAILROADS LIMITED. The legislature shall not authorize any county, township or municipal corporation to become indebted to aid in the construction or equipment of railroads to any amount that exceeds five percent of the value of the taxable property within that county, township or municipal corporation. The amount of taxable property shall be determined by the last assessment previous to the incurring of the indebtedness.

Sec. 13. SAFEKEEPING STATE FUNDS; SECURITY; DEPOSIT OF FUNDS; EMBEZZLEMENT. All officers and other persons charged with the safekeeping of state funds shall be required to give ample security for funds received by them and to keep an accurate entry of each sum received and of each payment and transfer.

If any person converts to his own use in any manner or form, or shall lend, with or without interest, or shall deposit in his own name, or otherwise than in the name of this state; or shall deposit in banks or with any person or persons or exchange for other funds or property, any portion of the funds of the state or the school funds aforesaid, except in the manner prescribed by law, every such act shall be and constitute an embezzlement of so much of the aforesaid state and school funds, or either of the same, as shall thus be taken, or loaned, or deposited or exchanged, and shall be a felony. Any failure to pay over, produce or account for the state school funds, or any part of the same entrusted to such officer or persons as by law required on demand, shall be held and be taken to be prima facie evidence of such embezzlement.

Sec. 14. ENVIRONMENT AND NATURAL RESOURCES FUND. A permanent environment and natural resources trust fund is established in the state treasury. Loans may be made of up to five percent of the principal of the fund for water system improvements as provided by law. The assets of the fund shall be appropriated by law for the public purpose of protection, conservation, preservation, and enhancement of the state's air, water, land, fish, wildlife, and other natural resources. The amount appropriated each year of a biennium, commencing on July 1 in each odd-numbered year and ending on and including June 30 in the next odd-numbered year, may be up to 5–1/2 percent of the market value of the fund on June 30 one year before the start of the biennium.

ARTICLE X—SPECIAL LEGISLATION; LOCAL GOVERNMENT

Section 1. PROHIBITION OF SPECIAL LEGISLATION; PARTICULAR SUBJECTS. In all cases when a general law can be made applicable, a special law shall not be enacted except as provided in section 2. Whether a general law could have been made applicable in any case shall be judicially determined without regard to any legislative assertion on that subject. The legislature shall pass no local or special law authorizing

- the laying out, opening, altering, vacating or maintaining of roads, highways, streets or alleys;

- remitting fines, penalties or forfeitures;

- changing the names of persons, places, lakes or rivers;

- authorizing the adoption or legitimation of children;

- changing the law of descent or succession;

- conferring rights on minors;

- declaring any named person of age;

- giving effect to informal or invalid wills or deeds, or affecting the estates of minors or persons under disability;

- granting divorces;

- exempting property from taxation or regulating the rate of interest on money;

- creating private corporations, or amending, renewing, or extending the charters thereof;

- granting to any private corporation, association, or individual any special or exclusive privilege, immunity or franchise whatever or authorizing public taxation for a private purpose.

The inhibitions of local or special laws in this section shall not prevent the passage of general laws on any of the subjects enumerated.

Sec. 2. SPECIAL LAWS; LOCAL GOVERNMENT. Every law which upon its effective date applies to a single local government unit or to a group of such units in a single county or a number of contiguous counties is a special law and shall name the unit or, in the latter case, the counties to which it applies. The legislature may enact special laws relating to local government units, but a special law, unless otherwise provided by general law, shall become effective only after its approval by the affected unit expressed through the voters or the governing body and by such majority as the legislature may direct. Any special law may be modified or superseded by a later home rule charter or amendment applicable to the same local government unit, but this does not prevent the adoption of subsequent laws on the same subject. The legislature may repeal any existing special or local law, but shall not amend, extend or modify any of the same except as provided in this section.

Sec. 3. LOCAL GOVERNMENT; LEGISLATION AFFECTING. The legislature may provide by law for the creation, organization, administration, consolidation, division and dissolution of local government units and their functions, for the change of boundaries thereof, for their elective and appointive officers including qualifications for office and for the transfer of county seats. A county boundary may not be changed or county seat transferred until approved in each county affected by a majority of the voters voting on the question.

Sec. 4. HOME RULE CHARTER. Any local government unit when authorized by law may adopt a home rule charter for its government. A charter shall become effective if approved by such majority of the voters of the local government unit as the legislature prescribes by general law. If a charter provides for the consolidation or separation of a city and a county, in whole or in part, it shall not be effective without approval of the voters both in the city and in the remainder of the county by the majority required by law.

Sec. 5. CHARTER COMMISSIONS. The legislature shall provide by law for charter commissions. Notwithstanding any other constitutional limitations the legislature may require that commission members be freeholders, provide for their appointment by judges of the district court, and permit any member to hold any other elective or appointive office other than judicial. Home rule charter amendments may be proposed by a charter commission or by a petition of five percent of the voters of the local government unit as determined by law and shall not become effective until approved by the voters by the majority required by law. Amendments may be proposed and adopted in any other manner provided by law. A local government unit may repeal its home rule charter and adopt a statutory form of government or a new charter upon the same majority vote as is required by law for the adoption of a charter in the first instance.

ARTICLE XI—MISCELLANEOUS SUBJECTS

Section 1. UNIFORM SYSTEM OF PUBLIC SCHOOLS. The stability of a republican form of government depending mainly upon the intelligence of the people, it is the duty of the legislature to establish a general and uniform system of public schools. The legislature shall make such provisions by taxation or otherwise as will secure a thorough and efficient system of public schools throughout the state.

Sec. 2. PROHIBITION AS TO AIDING SECTARIAN SCHOOL. In no case shall any public money or property be appropriated or used for the support of schools wherein the distinctive doctrines, creeds or tenets of any particular religious sect are promulgated or taught.

Sec. 3. STATE UNIVERSITY. All the rights, immunities, franchises and endowments heretofore granted or conferred upon the State University are perpetuated unto the university.

Sec. 4. LANDS TAKEN FOR PUBLIC WAY OR USE; COMPENSATION; COMMON CARRIERS. Land may be taken for public way and for the purpose of granting to any corporation the franchise of way for public use. In all cases, however, a fair and equitable compensation shall be paid for land and for the damages arising from taking it. All corporations which are common carriers enjoying the right of way in pursuance of the provisions of this section shall be bound to carry the mineral, agricultural and other productions of manufacturers on equal and reasonable terms.

Sec. 5. LOTTERIES. The legislature shall not authorize any lottery or the sale of lottery tickets, other than authorizing a lottery and sale of lottery tickets for a lottery operated by the state.

Sec. 6. PROHIBITION OF COMBINATIONS TO AFFECT MARKETS. Any combination of persons either as individuals or as members or officers of any corporation to monopolize markets for food products in this state or to interfere with, or restrict the freedom of markets is a criminal conspiracy and shall be punished as the legislature may provide.

Sec. 7. NO LICENSE REQUIRED TO PEDDLE. Any person may sell or peddle the products of the farm or garden occupied and cultivated by him without obtaining a license therefor.

Sec. 8. VETERANS' BONUS. The state may pay an adjusted compensation to persons who served in the armed forces of the United States during a period of war or armed conflict. Whenever authorized and in the amounts and on the terms fixed by law, the state may expend monies and pledge the public credit to provide money for the purposes of this section.

Sec. 9. MILITIA ORGANIZATION. The legislature shall pass laws necessary for the organization, discipline and service of the militia of the state.

Sec. 10. SEAT OF GOVERNMENT. The seat of government of the state shall be determined by law. The legislature may provide by law for a change of the seat of government by a vote of the people, or may locate the same upon the land granted by Congress for a seat of government. If the seat of government is changed, the capitol building and grounds shall be dedicated to an institution for the promotion of science, literature and the arts to be organized by the legislature of the state. The State Historical Society shall always be a department of this institution.

Sec. 11. STATE SEAL. A seal of the state shall be kept by the Governor and be used by him officially. It shall be called the Great Seal of the state.

Sec. 12. PRESERVATION OF HUNTING AND FISHING. Hunting and fishing and the taking of game and fish are a valued part of our heritage that shall be forever preserved for the people and shall be managed by law and regulation for the public good.

ARTICLE XII—PUBLIC HIGHWAY SYSTEM

Section 1. AUTHORITY OF STATE; PARTICIPATION OF POLITICAL SUBDIVISIONS. The state may construct, improve and maintain public highways, may assist political subdivisions in this work and by law may authorize any political subdivision to aid in highway work within its boundaries.

Sec. 2. TRUNK HIGHWAY SYSTEM. There is hereby created a trunk highway system which shall be constructed, improved and maintained as public highways by the state. The highways shall extend as nearly as possible along the routes described in any act of the legislature which has made or hereafter makes a route a part of the trunk highway system.

The legislature may add by law new routes to the trunk highway system.

Any route added by the legislature to the trunk highway system may be relocated or removed from the system as provided by law. The location of routes may be determined by boards, officers or tribunals in the manner prescribed by law.

Sec. 3. COUNTY STATE-AID HIGHWAY SYSTEM. A county state-aid highway system shall be constructed, improved and maintained by the counties as public highways in the manner provided by law. The system shall include streets in municipalities of fewer than 5,000 persons where necessary to provide an integrated and coordinated highway system and may include similar streets in larger municipalities.

Sec. 4. MUNICIPAL STATE-AID STREET SYSTEM. A municipal state-aid street system shall be constructed, improved and maintained as public highways by municipalities having a population of 5,000 or more in the manner provided by law.

Sec. 5. HIGHWAY USER TAX DISTRIBUTION FUND. There is hereby created a highway user tax distribution fund to be used solely for highway purposes as specified in this article. The fund consists of the proceeds of any taxes authorized by sections 9 and 10 of this article.

Sec. 6. TRUNK HIGHWAY FUND. There is hereby created a trunk highway fund which shall be used solely for the purposes specified in section 2 of this article and the payment of principal and interest of any bonds issued under the authority of section 11 of this article. All payments of principal and interest on bonds issued shall be a first charge on money coming into this fund during the year in which the principal or interest is payable.

Sec. 7. COUNTY STATE-AID HIGHWAY FUND. There is hereby created a county state-aid highway fund. The county state-aid highway fund shall be apportioned among the counties as provided by law. The funds apportioned shall be used by the counties as provided by law for aid in the construction, improvement and maintenance of county state-aid highways. The legislature may authorize the counties by law to use a part of the funds apportioned to them to aid in the construction, improvement and maintenance of other county highways, township roads, municipal streets and any other public highways, including but not limited to trunk highways and municipal state-aid streets within the respective counties.

Sec. 8. MUNICIPAL STATE-AID STREET FUND. There is hereby created a municipal state-aid street fund to be apportioned as provided by law among municipalities having a population of 5,000 or more. The fund shall be used by municipalities as provided by law for the construction, improvement and maintenance of municipal state-aid streets. The legislature may authorize municipalities to use a part of the fund in the construction, improvement and maintenance of other municipal streets, trunk highways, and county state-aid highways within the counties in which the municipality is located.

Sec. 9. TAXATION OF MOTOR VEHICLES. The legislature by law may tax motor vehicles using the public streets and highways on a more onerous basis than other personal property. Any such tax on motor vehicles shall be in lieu of all other taxes thereon, except wheelage taxes imposed by political subdivisions solely for highway purposes. The legislature may impose this tax on motor vehicles of companies paying taxes under the gross earnings system of taxation notwithstanding that earnings from the vehicles may be included in the earnings on which gross earnings taxes are computed. The proceeds of the tax shall be paid into the highway user tax distribution fund. The law may exempt from taxation any motor vehicle owned by a nonresident of the state properly licensed in another state and transiently or temporarily using the streets and highways of the state.

Sec. 10. TAXATION OF MOTOR FUEL. The legislature may levy an excise tax on any means or substance used for propelling vehicles on the public highways of this state or on the business of selling it. The proceeds of the tax shall be paid into the highway user tax distribution fund.

Sec. 11. HIGHWAY BONDS. The legislature may provide by law for the sale of bonds to carry out the provisions of section 2. The proceeds shall be paid into the trunk highway fund. Any bonds shall mature serially over a term not exceeding 20 years and shall not be sold for less than par and accrued interest. If the trunk highway fund is not adequate to pay principal and interest of these bonds when due, the legislature may levy on all taxable property of the state in an amount sufficient to meet the deficiency or it may appropriate to the fund money in the state treasury not otherwise appropriated.

Appendix III

The Constitution of The United States, Old Form

Preamble

We the people of the United States, in order to form a more perfect union, establish justice, insure domestic tranquility, provide for the common defense, promote the general welfare, and secure the blessings of liberty to ourselves and our posterity, do ordain and establish this Constitution for the United States of America.

Article I

Section 1. All legislative powers herein granted shall be vested in a Congress of the United States, which shall consist of a Senate and House of Representatives.

Section 2. The House of Representatives shall be composed of members chosen every second year by the people of the several states, and the electors in each state shall have the qualifications requisite for electors of the most numerous branch of the state legislature.

No person shall be a Representative who shall not have attained to the age of twenty five years, and been seven years a citizen of the United States, and who shall not, when elected, be an inhabitant of that state in which he shall be chosen.

Representatives and direct taxes shall be apportioned among the several states which may be included within this union, according to their respective numbers, which shall be determined by adding to the whole number of free persons, including those bound to service for a term of years, and excluding Indians not taxed, three fifths of all other Persons [see Amendment XIV]. The actual Enumeration shall be made within three years after the first meeting of the Congress of the United States, and within every subsequent term of ten years, in such manner as they shall by law direct. The number of Representatives shall not exceed one for every thirty thousand, but each state shall have at least one Representative; and until such enumeration shall be made, the state of New Hampshire shall be entitled to chuse three, Massachusetts eight, Rhode Island and Providence Plantations one, Connecticut five, New York six, New Jersey four, Pennsylvania eight, Delaware one, Maryland six, Virginia ten, North Carolina five, South Carolina five, and Georgia three.

When vacancies happen in the Representation from any state, the executive authority thereof shall issue writs of election to fill such vacancies.

The House of Representatives shall choose their speaker and other officers; and shall have the sole power of impeachment.

Section 3. The Senate of the United States shall be composed of two Senators from each state, chosen by the legislature thereof [see Amendment XVII], for six years; and each Senator shall have one vote.

Immediately after they shall be assembled in consequence of the first election, they shall be divided as equally as may be into three classes. The seats of the Senators of the first class shall be vacated at the expiration of the second year, of the second class at the expiration of the fourth year, and the third class at the expiration of the sixth year, so that one third may be chosen every second year; and if vacancies happen by resignation [see Amendment XVII], or otherwise, during the recess of the legislature of any state, the executive thereof may make temporary appointments until the next meeting of the legislature, which shall then fill such vacancies.

No person shall be a Senator who shall not have attained to the age of thirty years, and been nine years a citizen of the United States and who shall not, when elected, be an inhabitant of that state for which he shall be chosen.

The Vice President of the United States shall be President of the Senate, but shall have no vote, unless they be equally divided.

The Senate shall choose their other officers, and also a President pro tempore, in the absence of the Vice President, or when he shall exercise the office of President of the United States.

The Senate shall have the sole power to try all impeachments. When sitting for that purpose, they shall be on oath or affirmation. When the President of the United States is tried, the Chief Justice shall preside: And no person shall be convicted without the concurrence of two thirds of the members present.

Judgment in cases of impeachment shall not extend further than to removal from office, and disqualification to hold and enjoy any office of honor, trust or profit under the United States: but the party convicted shall nevertheless be liable and subject to indictment, trial, judgment and punishment, according to law.

Section 4. The times, places and manner of holding elections for Senators and Representatives, shall be prescribed in each state by the legislature thereof; but the Congress may at any time by law make or alter such regulations, except as to the places of choosing Senators [see Amendment XVII] .

The Congress shall assemble at least once in every year, and such meeting shall be on the first Monday in December, unless they shall by law appoint a different day.

Section 5. Each House shall be the judge of the elections, returns and qualifications of its own members, and a majority of each shall constitute a quorum to do business; but a smaller number may adjourn from day to day, and may be authorized to compel the attendance of absent members, in such manner, and under such penalties as each House may provide.

Each House may determine the rules of its proceedings, punish its members for disorderly behavior, and, with the concurrence of two thirds, expel a member.

Each House shall keep a journal of its proceedings, and from time to time publish the same, excepting such parts as may in their judgment require secrecy; and the yeas and nays of the members of either House on any question shall, at the desire of one fifth of those present, be entered on the journal.

Neither House, during the session of Congress, shall, without the consent of the other, adjourn for more than three days, nor to any other place than that in which the two Houses shall be sitting.

Section 6. The Senators and Representatives shall receive a compensation for their services, to be ascertained by law, and paid out of the treasury of the United States. They shall in all cases, except treason, felony and breach of the peace, be privileged from arrest during their attendance at the session of their respective Houses, and in going to and returning from the same; and for any speech or debate in either House, they shall not be questioned in any other place.

No Senator or Representative shall, during the time for which he was elected, be appointed to any civil office under the authority of the United States, which shall have been created, or the emoluments whereof shall have been increased during such time: and no person holding any office under the United States, shall be a member of either House during his continuance in office.

Section 7. All bills for raising revenue shall originate in the House of Representatives; but the Senate may propose or concur with amendments as on other Bills.

Every bill which shall have passed the House of Representatives and the Senate, shall, before it become a law, be presented to the President of the United States; if he approve he shall sign it, but if not he shall return it, with his objections to that House in which it shall have originated, who shall enter the objections at large on their journal, and proceed to reconsider it. If after such reconsideration two thirds of that House shall agree to pass the bill, it shall be sent, together with the objections, to the other House, by which it shall likewise be reconsidered, and if approved by two thirds of that House, it shall become a law. But in all such cases the votes of both Houses shall be determined by yeas and nays, and the names of the persons voting for and against the bill shall be entered on the journal of each House respectively. If any bill shall not be returned by the President within ten days (Sundays excepted) after it shall have been presented to him, the same shall be a law, in like manner as if he had signed it, unless the Congress by their adjournment prevent its return, in which case it shall not be a law.

Every order, resolution, or vote to which the concurrence of the Senate and House of Representatives may be necessary (except on a question of adjournment) shall be presented to the President of the United States; and before the same shall take effect, shall be approved by him, or being disapproved by him, shall be repassed by two thirds of the Senate and House of Representatives, according to the rules and limitations prescribed in the case of a bill.

Section 8. The Congress shall have power:
To lay and collect taxes, duties, imposts and excises, to pay the debts and provide for the common defense and general welfare of the United States; but all duties, imposts and excises shall be uniform throughout the United States;

To borrow money on the credit of the United States;

To regulate commerce with foreign nations, and among the several states, and with the Indian tribes;

To establish a uniform rule of naturalization, and uniform laws on the subject of bankruptcies throughout the United States;

To coin money, regulate the value thereof, and of foreign coin, and fix the standard of weights and measures;

To provide for the punishment of counterfeiting the securities and current coin of the United States;

To establish post offices and post roads;

To promote the progress of science and useful arts, by securing for limited times to authors and inventors the exclusive right to their respective writings and discoveries;

To constitute tribunals inferior to the Supreme Court;

To define and punish piracies and felonies committed on the high seas, and offenses against the law of nations;

To declare war, grant letters of marque and reprisal, and make rules concerning captures on land and water;

To raise and support armies, but no appropriation of money to that use shall be for a longer term than two years;

To provide and maintain a navy;

To make rules for the government and regulation of the land and naval forces;

To provide for calling forth the militia to execute the laws of the union, suppress insurrections and repel invasions;

To provide for organizing, arming, and disciplining, the militia, and for governing such part of them as may be employed in the service of the United States, reserving to the states respectively, the appointment of the officers, and the authority of training the militia according to the discipline prescribed by Congress;

To exercise exclusive legislation in all cases whatsoever, over such District (not exceeding ten miles square) as may, by cession of particular states, and the acceptance of Congress, become the seat of the government of the United States, and to exercise like authority over all places purchased by the consent of the legislature of the state in which the same shall be, for the erection of forts, magazines, arsenals, dockyards, and other needful buildings; —And

To make all laws which shall be necessary and proper for carrying into execution The foregoing powers, and all other powers vested by this Constitution in the government of the United States, or in any department or officer thereof.

Section 9. The migration or importation of such persons as any of the states now existing shall think proper to admit, shall not be prohibited by the Congress prior to the year one thousand eight hundred and eight, but a tax or duty may be imposed on such importation, not exceeding ten dollars for each person.

The privilege of the writ of habeas corpus shall not be suspended, unless when in cases of rebellion or invasion the public safety may require it.

No bill of attainder or ex post facto Law shall be passed.

No capitation, or other direct, tax shall be laid, unless in proportion to the census or enumeration herein before directed to be taken [see Amendment XVI] .

No tax or duty shall be laid on articles exported from any state.

No preference shall be given by any regulation of commerce or revenue to the ports of one state over those of another: nor shall vessels bound to, or from, one state, be obliged to enter, clear or pay duties in another.

No money shall be drawn from the treasury, but in consequence of appropriations made by law; and a regular statement and account of receipts and expenditures of all public money shall be published from time to time.

No title of nobility shall be granted by the United States: and no person holding any office of profit or trust under them, shall, without the consent of the Congress, accept of any present, emolument, office, or title, of any kind whatever, from any king, prince, or foreign state.

Section 10. No state shall enter into any treaty, alliance, or confederation; grant letters of marque and reprisal; coin money; emit bills of credit; make anything but gold and silver coin a tender in payment of debts; pass any bill of attainder, ex post facto law, or law impairing the obligation of contracts, or grant any title of nobility.

No state shall, without the consent of the Congress, lay any imposts or duties on imports or exports, except what may be absolutely necessary for executing its inspection laws: and the net produce of all duties and imposts, laid by any state on imports or exports, shall be for the use of the treasury of the United States; and all such laws shall be subject to the revision and control of the Congress.

No state shall, without the consent of Congress, lay any duty of tonnage, keep troops, or ships of war in time of peace, enter into any agreement or compact with another state, or with a foreign power, or engage in war, unless actually invaded, or in such imminent danger as will not admit of delay.

Article II

Section 1. The executive power shall be vested in a President of the United States of America. He shall hold his office during the term of four years, and, together with the Vice President, chosen for the same term, be elected, as follows:

Each state shall appoint, in such manner as the Legislature thereof may direct, a number of electors, equal to the whole number of Senators and Representatives to which the State may be entitled in the Congress: but no Senator or Representative, or person holding an office of trust or profit under the United States, shall be appointed an elector.

The electors [see Amendment XII] shall meet in their respective states, and vote by ballot for two persons, of whom one at least shall not be an inhabitant of the same state with themselves. And they shall make a list of all the persons voted for, and of the number of votes for each; which list they shall sign and certify, and transmit sealed to the seat of the government of the United

States, directed to the President of the Senate. The President of the Senate shall, in the presence of the Senate and House of Representatives, open all the certificates, and the votes shall then be counted. The person having the greatest number of votes shall be the President, if such number be a majority of the whole number of electors appointed; and if there be more than one who have such majority, and have an equal number of votes, then the House of Representatives shall immediately choose by ballot one of them for President; and if no person have a majority, then from the five highest on the list the said House shall in like manner choose the President. But in choosing the President, the votes shall be taken by States, the representation from each state having one vote; A quorum for this purpose shall consist of a member or members from two thirds of the states, and a majority of all the states shall be necessary to a choice. In every case, after the choice of the President, the person having the greatest number of votes of the electors shall be the Vice President. But if there should remain two or more who have equal votes, the Senate shall choose from them by ballot the Vice President.

The Congress may determine the time of choosing the electors, and the day on which they shall give their votes; which day shall be the same throughout the United States.

No person except a natural born citizen, or a citizen of the United States, at the time of the adoption of this Constitution, shall be eligible to the office of President; neither shall any person be eligible to that office who shall not have attained to the age of thirty five years, and been fourteen Years a resident within the United States.

In case of the removal of the President from office [see Amendment XXV], or of his death, resignation, or inability to discharge the powers and duties of the said office, the same shall devolve on the Vice President, and the Congress may by law provide for the case of removal, death, resignation or inability, both of the President and Vice President, declaring what officer shall then act as President, and such officer shall act accordingly, until the disability be removed, or a President shall be elected.

The President shall, at stated times, receive for his services, a compensation, which shall neither be increased nor diminished during the period for which he shall have been elected, and he shall not receive within that period any other emolument from the United States, or any of them.

Before he enter on the execution of his office, he shall take the following oath or affirmation:—"I do solemnly swear (or affirm) that I will faithfully execute the office of President of the United States, and will to the best of my ability, preserve, protect and defend the Constitution of the United States."

Section 2. The President shall be commander in chief of the Army and Navy of the United States, and of the militia of the several states, when called into the actual service of the United States; he may require the opinion, in writing, of the principal officer in each of the executive departments, upon any subject relating to the duties of their respective offices, and he shall have power to grant reprieves and pardons for offenses against the United States, except in cases of impeachment.

He shall have power, by and with the advice and consent of the Senate, to make treaties, provided two thirds of the Senators present concur; and he shall nominate, and by and with the advice and consent of the Senate, shall appoint ambassadors, other public ministers and consuls, judges of the Supreme Court, and all other officers of the United States, whose appointments are not herein otherwise provided for, and which shall be established by law: but the Congress may by law vest the appointment of such inferior officers, as they think proper, in the President alone, in the courts of law, or in the heads of departments.

The President shall have power to fill up all vacancies that may happen during the recess of the Senate, by granting commissions which shall expire at the end of their next session.

Section 3. He shall from time to time give to the Congress information of the state of the union, and recommend to their consideration such measures as he shall judge necessary and expedient; he may, on extraordinary occasions, convene both Houses, or either of them, and in case of disagreement between them, with respect to the time of adjournment, he may adjourn them to such time as he shall think proper; he shall receive ambassadors and other public ministers; he shall take care that the laws be faithfully executed, and shall commission all the officers of the United States.

Section 4. The President, Vice President and all civil officers of the United States, shall be removed from office on impeachment for, and conviction of, treason, bribery, or other high crimes and misdemeanors.

Article III

Section 1. The judicial power of the United States, shall be vested in one Supreme Court, and in such inferior courts as the Congress may from time to time ordain and establish. The judges, both of the supreme and inferior courts, shall hold their offices during good behaviour, and shall, at stated times, receive for their services, a compensation, which shall not be diminished during their continuance in office.

Section 2. The judicial power shall extend

—to all cases, in law and equity, arising under this
   Constitution, the laws of the United States, and

treaties made, or which shall be made, under their authority;

—to all cases affecting ambassadors, other public ministers and consuls;

—to all cases of admiralty and maritime jurisdiction;

—to controversies to which the United States shall be a party;

—to controversies between two or more states;

—between a state and citizens of another state [see Amendment XI];

—between citizens of different states;

—between citizens of the same state claiming lands under grants of different states, and between a state, or the citizens thereof, and foreign states, citizens or subjects.

In all cases affecting ambassadors, other public ministers and consuls, and those in which a state shall be party, the Supreme Court shall have original jurisdiction. In all the other cases before mentioned, the Supreme Court shall have appellate jurisdiction, both as to law and fact, with such exceptions, and under such regulations as the Congress shall make.

The trial of all crimes, except in cases of impeachment, shall be by jury; and such trial shall be held in the state where the said crimes shall have been committed; but when not committed within any state, the trial shall be at such place or places as the Congress may by law have directed.

Section 3. Treason against the United States, shall consist only in levying war against them, or in adhering to their enemies, giving them aid and comfort. No person shall be convicted of treason unless on the testimony of two witnesses to the same overt act, or on confession in open court.

The Congress shall have power to declare the punishment of treason, but no attainder of treason shall work corruption of blood, or forfeiture except during the life of the person attainted.

Article IV

Section 1. Full faith and credit shall be given in each state to the public acts, records, and judicial proceedings of every other state. And the Congress may by general laws prescribe the manner in which such acts, records, and proceedings shall be proved, and the effect thereof.

Section 2. The citizens of each state shall be entitled to all privileges and immunities of citizens in the several states.

A person charged in any state with treason, felony, or other crime, who shall flee from justice, and be found in another state, shall on demand of the executive authority of the state from which he fled, be delivered up, to be removed to the state having jurisdiction of the crime.

No person held to service or labor [see Amendment XIII] in one state, under the laws thereof, escaping into another, shall, in consequence of any law or regulation therein, be discharged from such service or labor, but shall be delivered up on claim of the party to whom such service or labor may be due.

Section 3. New states may be admitted by the Congress into this union; but no new states shall be formed or erected within the jurisdiction of any other state; nor any state be formed by the junction of two or more states, or parts of states, without the consent of the legislatures of the states concerned as well as of the Congress.

The Congress shall have power to dispose of and make all needful rules and regulations respecting the territory or other property belonging to the United States; and nothing in this Constitution shall be so construed as to prejudice any claims of the United States, or of any particular state.

Section 4. The United States shall guarantee to every state in this union a republican form of government, and shall protect each of them against invasion; and on application of the legislature, or of the executive (when the legislature cannot be convened) against domestic violence.

Article V
The Congress, whenever two thirds of both houses shall deem it necessary, shall propose amendments to this Constitution, or, on the application of the legislatures of two thirds of the several states, shall call a convention for proposing amendments, which, in either case, shall be valid to all intents and purposes, as part of this Constitution, when ratified by the legislatures of three fourths of the several states, or by conventions in three fourths thereof, as the one or the other mode of ratification may be proposed by the Congress; provided that no amendment which may be made prior to the year one thousand eight hundred and eight shall in any manner affect the first and fourth clauses in the ninth section of the first article; and that no state, without its consent, shall be deprived of its equal suffrage in the Senate.

Article VI
All debts contracted and engagements entered into, before the adoption of this Constitution, shall be as valid against the United States under this Constitution, as under the Confederation.

This Constitution, and the laws of the United States which shall be made in pursuance thereof; and all treaties made, or which shall be made, under the authority of the United States, shall be the supreme law of the land; and the judges in every state shall be bound thereby, anything in the Constitution or laws of any State to the contrary notwithstanding.

The Senators and Representatives before mentioned, and the members of the several state legislatures, and all executive and judicial officers, both of the United States and of the several states, shall be bound by oath or affirmation, to support this Constitution; but no religious test shall ever be required as a qualification to any office or public trust under the United States.

Article VII

The ratification of the conventions of nine states, shall be sufficient for the establishment of this Constitution between the states so ratifying the same.

Done in convention by the unanimous consent of the states present the seventeenth day of September in the year of our Lord one thousand seven hundred and eighty seven and of the independence of the United States of America the twelfth.

Amendments
Amendment I

Congress shall make no law respecting an establishment of religion, or prohibiting the free exercise thereof; or abridging the freedom of speech, or of the press; or the right of the people peaceably to assemble, and to petition the government for a redress of grievances.

Amendment II

A well regulated militia, being necessary to the security of a free state, the right of the people to keep and bear arms, shall not be infringed.

Amendment III

No soldier shall, in time of peace be quartered in any house, without the consent of the owner, nor in time of war, but in a manner to be prescribed by law.

Amendment IV

The right of the people to be secure in their persons, houses, papers, and effects, against unreasonable searches and seizures, shall not be violated, and no warrants shall issue, but upon probable cause, supported by oath or affirmation, and particularly describing the place to be searched, and the persons or things to be seized.

Amendment V

No person shall be held to answer for a capital, or otherwise infamous crime, unless on a presentment or indictment of a grand jury, except in cases arising in the land or naval forces, or in the militia, when in actual service in time of war or public danger; nor shall any person be subject for the same offense to be twice put in jeopardy of life or limb; nor shall be compelled in any criminal case to be a witness against himself, nor be deprived of life, liberty, or property, without due process of law; nor shall private property be taken for public use, without just compensation.

Amendment VI

In all criminal prosecutions, the accused shall enjoy the right to a speedy and public trial, by an impartial jury of the state and district wherein the crime shall have been committed, which district shall have been previously ascertained by law, and to be informed of the nature and cause of the accusation; to be confronted with the witnesses against him; to have compulsory process for obtaining witnesses in his favor, and to have the assistance of counsel for his defense.

Amendment VII

In suits at common law, where the value in controversy shall exceed twenty dollars, the right of trial by jury shall be preserved, and no fact tried by a jury, shall be otherwise reexamined in any court of the United States, than according to the rules of the common law.

Amendment VIII

Excessive bail shall not be required, nor excessive fines imposed, nor cruel and unusual punishments inflicted.

Amendment IX

The enumeration in the Constitution, of certain rights, shall not be construed to deny or disparage others retained by the people.

Amendment X

The powers not delegated to the United States by the Constitution, nor prohibited by it to the states, are reserved to the states respectively, or to the people.

Amendment XI

The judicial power of the United States shall not be construed to extend to any suit in law or equity, commenced or prosecuted against one of the United States by citizens of another state, or by citizens or subjects of any foreign state.

Amendment XII

The electors shall meet in their respective states and vote by ballot for President and Vice-President, one of whom, at least, shall not be an inhabitant of the same state with themselves; they shall name in their ballots the person voted for as President, and in distinct ballots the person voted for as Vice-President, and they shall make distinct lists of all persons voted for as President, and of all persons voted for as Vice-President, and of the number of votes for each, which lists they shall sign and certify, and transmit sealed to the seat of the government of the United States, directed to the President of the Senate;

—The President of the Senate shall, in the presence of the Senate and House of Representatives, open all the certificates and the votes shall then be counted;

—The person having the greatest number of votes for President, shall be the President, if such number be a majority of the whole number of electors appointed; and if no person have such majority, then from the persons having the highest numbers not exceeding three on the list of those voted for as President, the House of Representatives shall choose immediately, by ballot, the President. But in choosing the President, the votes shall be taken by states, the representation from each state having one vote; a quorum for this purpose shall consist of a member or members from two-thirds of the states, and a majority of all the states shall be necessary to a choice [see Amendment XX]. And if the House of Representatives shall not choose a President whenever the right of choice shall devolve upon them, before the fourth day of March next following, then the Vice-President shall act as President, as in the case of the death or other constitutional disability of the President. The person having the greatest number of votes as Vice-President, shall be the Vice-President, if such number be a majority of the whole number of electors appointed, and if no person have a majority, then from the two highest numbers on the list, the Senate shall choose the Vice-President; a quorum for the purpose shall consist of two-thirds of the whole number of

Senators, and a majority of the whole number shall be necessary to a choice. But no person constitutionally ineligible to the office of President shall be eligible to that of Vice-President of the United States.

Amendment XIII

Section 1. Neither slavery nor involuntary servitude, except as a punishment for crime whereof the party shall have been duly convicted, shall exist within the United States, or any place subject to their jurisdiction.

Section 2. Congress shall have power to enforce this article by appropriate legislation.

Amendment XIV

Section 1. All persons born or naturalized in the United States, and subject to the jurisdiction thereof, are citizens of the United States and of the state wherein they reside. No state shall make or enforce any law which shall abridge the privileges or immunities of citizens of the United States; nor shall any state deprive any person of life, liberty, or property, without due process of law; nor deny to any person within its jurisdiction the equal protection of the laws.

Section 2. Representatives shall be apportioned among the several states according to their respective numbers, counting the whole number of persons in each state, excluding Indians not taxed. But when the right to vote at any election for the choice of electors for President and Vice President of the United States, Representatives in Congress, the executive and judicial officers of a state, or the members of the legislature thereof, is denied to any of the male inhabitants of such state [see Amendment XIX], being twenty-one years of age [see Amendment XXVI], and citizens of the United States, or in any way abridged, except for participation in rebellion, or other crime, the basis of representation therein shall be reduced in the proportion which the number of such male citizens shall bear to the whole number of male citizens twenty-one years of age in such state.

Section 3. No person shall be a Senator or Representative in Congress, or elector of President and Vice President, or hold any office, civil or military, under the United States, or under any state, who, having previously taken an oath, as a member of Congress, or as an officer of the United States, or as a member of any state legislature, or as an executive or judicial officer of any state, to support the Constitution of the United States, shall have engaged in insurrection or rebellion against the same, or given aid or comfort to the enemies thereof. But Congress may by a vote of two-thirds of each House, remove such disability.

Section 4. The validity of the public debt of the United States, authorized by law, including debts incurred for payment of pensions and bounties for services in suppressing insurrection or rebellion, shall not be questioned. But neither the United States nor any state shall assume or pay any debt or obligation incurred in aid of insurrection or rebellion against the United States, or any claim for the loss or emancipation of any slave; but all such debts, obligations and claims shall be held illegal and void.

Section 5. The Congress shall have power to enforce, by appropriate legislation, the provisions of this article.

Amendment XV
Section 1. The right of citizens of the United States to vote shall not be denied or abridged by the United States or by any state on account of race, color, or previous condition of servitude.

Section 2. The Congress shall have power to enforce this article by appropriate legislation.

Amendment XVI

The Congress shall have power to lay and collect taxes on incomes, from whatever source derived, without apportionment among the several states, and without regard to any census or enumeration.

Amendment XVII

The Senate of the United States shall be composed of two Senators from each state, elected by the people thereof, for six years; and each Senator shall have one vote. The electors in each state shall have the qualifications requisite for electors of the most numerous branch of the state legislatures.

When vacancies happen in the representation of any state in the Senate, the executive authority of such state shall issue writs of election to fill such vacancies: Provided, that the legislature of any state may empower the executive thereof to make temporary appointments until the people fill the vacancies by election as the legislature may direct.

This amendment shall not be so construed as to affect the election or term of any Senator chosen before it becomes valid as part of the Constitution.

Amendment XVIII [see Amendment XXI]

Section 1. After one year from the ratification of this article the manufacture, sale, or transportation of intoxicating liquors within, the importation thereof into, or the exportation thereof from the United States and all territory subject to the jurisdiction thereof for beverage purposes is hereby prohibited.

Section 2. The Congress and the several states shall have concurrent power to enforce this article by appropriate legislation.

Section 3. This article shall be inoperative unless it shall have been ratified as an amendment to the Constitution by the legislatures of the several states, as provided in the Constitution, within seven years from the date of the submission hereof to the states by the Congress.

Amendment XIX

The right of citizens of the United States to vote shall not be denied or abridged by the United States or by any state on account of sex.

Congress shall have power to enforce this article by appropriate legislation.

Amendment XX

Section 1. The terms of the President and Vice President shall end at noon on the 20th day of January, and the terms of Senators and Representatives at noon on the 3d day of January, of the years in which such terms would have ended if this article had not been ratified; and the terms of their successors shall then begin.

Section 2. The Congress shall assemble at least once in every year, and such meeting shall begin at noon on the 3d day of January, unless they shall by law appoint a different day.

Section 3. If, at the time fixed for the beginning of the term of the President, the President elect shall have died, the Vice President elect shall become President [see Amendment XXV]. If a President shall not have been chosen before the time fixed for the beginning of his term, or if the President elect shall have failed to qualify, then the Vice President elect shall act as President until a President shall have qualified; and the Congress may by law provide for the case wherein neither a President elect nor a Vice President elect shall have qualified, declaring who shall then act as President, or the manner in which one who is to act shall be selected, and such person shall act accordingly until a President or Vice President shall have qualified.

Section 4. The Congress may by law provide for the case of the death of any of the persons from whom the House of

Representatives may choose a President whenever the right of choice shall have devolved upon them, and for the case of the death of any of the persons from whom the Senate may choose a Vice President whenever the right of choice shall have devolved upon them.

Section 5. Sections 1 and 2 shall take effect on the 15th day of October following the ratification of this article.

Section 6. This article shall be inoperative unless it shall have been ratified as an amendment to the Constitution by the legislatures of three-fourths of the several states within seven years from the date of its submission.

Amendment XXI

Section 1. The eighteenth article of amendment to the Constitution of the United States is hereby repealed.

Section 2. The transportation or importation into any state, territory, or possession of the United States for delivery or use therein of intoxicating liquors, in violation of the laws thereof, is hereby prohibited.

Section 3. This article shall be inoperative unless it shall have been ratified as an amendment to the Constitution by conventions in the several states, as provided in the Constitution, within seven years from the date of the submission hereof to the states by the Congress.

Amendment XXII

Section 1. No person shall be elected to the office of the President more than twice, and no person who has held the office of President, or acted as President, for more than two years of a term to which some other person was elected President shall be elected to the office of the President more than once. But this article shall not apply to any person holding the office of President when this article was proposed by the Congress, and shall not prevent any person who may be holding the office of President, or acting as President, during the term within which this article becomes operative from holding the office of President or acting as President during the remainder of such term.

Section 2. This article shall be inoperative unless it shall have been ratified as an amendment to the Constitution by the legislatures of three-fourths of the several states within seven years from the date of its submission to the states by the Congress.

Amendment XXIII

Section 1. The District constituting the seat of government of the United States shall appoint in such manner as the Congress may direct:

A number of electors of President and Vice President equal to the whole number of Senators and Representatives in Congress to which the District would be entitled if it were a state, but in no event more than the least populous state; they shall be in addition to those appointed by the states, but they shall be considered, for the purposes of the election of President and Vice President, to be electors appointed by a state; and they shall meet in the District and perform such duties as provided by the twelfth article of amendment.

Section 2. The Congress shall have power to enforce this article by appropriate legislation.

Amendment XXIV

Section 1. The right of citizens of the United States to vote in any primary or other election for President or Vice President, for electors for President or Vice President, or for Senator or Representative in Congress, shall not be denied or abridged by the United States or any state by reason of failure to pay any poll tax or other tax.

Section 2. The Congress shall have power to enforce this article by appropriate legislation.

Amendment XXV

Section 1. In case of the removal of the President from office or of his death or resignation, the Vice President shall become President.

Section 2. Whenever there is a vacancy in the office of the Vice President, the President shall nominate a Vice President who shall take office upon confirmation by a majority vote of both Houses of Congress.

Section 3. Whenever the President transmits to the President pro tempore of the Senate and the Speaker of the House of Representatives his written declaration that he is unable to discharge the powers and duties of his office, and until he transmits to them a written declaration to the contrary, such powers and duties shall be discharged by the Vice President as Acting President.

Section 4. Whenever the Vice President and a majority of either the principal officers of the executive departments or of such other body as Congress may by law provide, transmit to the President pro tempore of the Senate and the Speaker of the House of Representatives their written declaration that the President is unable to discharge the powers and duties of his office, the Vice President shall immediately assume the powers and duties of the office as Acting President.

Thereafter, when the President transmits to the President pro tempore of the Senate and the Speaker of the House of Representatives his written declaration that no inability exists, he shall resume the powers and duties of his office unless the Vice President and a majority of either the principal officers of the executive department or of such other body as Congress may by law provide, transmit within four days to the President pro tempore of the Senate and the Speaker of the House of Representatives their written declaration that the President is unable to discharge the powers and duties of his office. Thereupon Congress shall decide the issue, assembling within forty-eight hours for that purpose if not in session. If the Congress, within twenty-one days after receipt of the latter written declaration, or, if Congress is not in session, within twenty-one days after Congress is required to assemble, determines by two-thirds vote of both Houses that the President is unable to discharge the powers and duties of his office, the Vice President shall continue to discharge the same as Acting President; otherwise, the President shall resume the powers and duties of his office.

Amendment XXVI

Section 1. The right of citizens of the United States, who are 18 years of age or older, to vote, shall not be denied or abridged by the United States or any state on account of age.

Section 2. The Congress shall have the power to enforce this article by appropriate legislation.

Amendment XXVII

No law, varying the compensation for the services of the Senators and Representatives, shall take effect, until an election of Representatives shall have intervened.

Appendix IV

Resources for Responsible Government on the World Wide Web

Here some of the best links available on the Internet on responsible government. I am always looking for truly first-class Web pages on this subject, so if you know the URL for any send me an e-mail (responsegov@geocities.com) and I'll have a look.

UNITED KINGDOM PARLIAMENT

The Palace of Westminster is the home of the Mother of Parliaments, and the official British Parliament Web site is the Mother Lode of Parliamentary information, all from the original source. The main Parliamentary site is mirrored at Her Majesty's Stationery Office (HMSO) Web site.

The British Parliament is, of course, divided into the hereditary and appointive House of Lords and the elective House of Commons The Parliament site has a comprehensive index, a well-thought-out guide, and the ever-popular CGI-BIN powered site search engine.

Hansard's is the parliamentary equivalent (British and others) of the U.S. *Congressional Record*, but one read of each publication will show the sea-difference between the two systems. The HMSO site has the current Hansard of the most recent debates in the

House of Commons. Here you will get the word-for-word record of what happens on the floor of the Commons; the phrase "read into the record as extensions of remarks" which appears regularly in the *Congressional Record* does not happen in Hansard.

If you have more questions you can direct them to Parliament's Enquiries section. British politics junkies will want to hop over to the United Kingdom Politics and the Blake's Parliamentary Web sites. Those who missed the old Parliamentary Channel web site can now rejoice—there is now a live streaming video feed of the House of Commons

Official British Parliament Web site:
http://www.parliament.uk

British Parliament mirror site at H.M. Stationery Office:
http://www.parliament.the-stationery-office.co.uk

House of Lords
http://www.parliament.the-stationery-
office.co.uk/pa/ld/ldhome.htm

House of Commons
http://www.parliament.uk/commons/HSECOM.HTM.

Current Hansard:
http://www.parliament.the-stationery-
office.co.uk/pa/cm/cmhansrd.htm

Parliamentary Enquiries:
http://www.parliament.uk/parliament/PAENQ.HTM

United Kingdom Politics Web site:
http://www.ukpol.co.uk

Blake's Parliamentary Web site:
http://www.blakeuk.com/parliament/index.shtml

Live streaming video of the House of Commons:
http://www.westminster-digital.co.uk/parliament/

PARLIAMENT OF CANADA

The many Web sites of the Government of Canada and the 36th Parliament of Canada are clean, well-designed, load quickly, and are chock-a-block with first-class data.

But far and away the crown jewel of the Canadian Government site is Hon. Eugene A. Forsey's (1904–1991) explanations of *How Canadians Govern Themselves.* Senator Forsey's text has the clarity of Waterford crystal and the succinctness of a master's touch. Forsey's chapters on "Parliamentary Government" and "What Goes on in Parliament" are the clearest explanation of how the process works north of the 49th Parallel, and how government ought to work south of the 49th. Forsey's "Canadian and American Government" is a withering critique of the "separation of powers" fallacy. Also useful is his chapter on Canadian federal institutions the Sovereign, the Governor-General, the Lieutenant-Governors of the Provinces, and the Federal and Provincial Parliaments.

There are also Web sites for the Governor-General of Canada and Prime Minister Jean Chrétien of Canada. You should also check out the link to the *Charter of Rights and Freedoms.* The Charter is a "bill of rights" written in as "positive statements," rather than the American Bill of Rights which are written in as "negative" statements ("Congress shall pass no law…")

Canada's Provinces and Territories stretch *ad mari usque ad mare* ("from sea to sea," the national motto), and all have Web sites. From the Pacific to the Atlantic are British Columbia, Alberta, Saskatchewan, Manitoba, Ontario, Quebec, New Brunswick, Nova Scotia, Prince Edward Island and Newfoundland. In the far, far north are the three Territories of the Yukon, the Northwest Territories and the brand new (officialy started 1 April 1999) Territory of Nunavut, which faces Greenland. Fans of the Inuktitut language will want to download the new Nunacom font of the Inuktitut alphabet, one of four official languages of the Territory. Be the first on your block to send a secret message in Inuktitut.

Government of Canada official Web site:
http://canada.gc.ca/

36th Parliament of Canada:
http://www.parl.gc.ca/36/main-e.htm

Sen. Eugene Forsey, "How Canadians Govern Themselves":
http://www.parl.gc.ca/36/refmat/library/forsey/how-e.htm.

Sen. Eugene Forsey, "Parliamentary Government":
http://www.parl.gc.ca/36/refmat/library/forsey/parlgov-e.htm

Sen. Eugene Forsey, "What Goes On in Parliament":
http://www.parl.gc.ca/36/refmat/library/forsey/parl-e.htm

Sen Eugene Forsey, "Canadian and American Government":
http://www.parl.gc.ca/36/refmat/library/forsey/canus-e.htm

Sen. Eugene Forsey, "Canadian Federal Institutions":
http://www.parl.gc.ca/36/refmat/library/forsey/fedinst-e.htm

Governor General of Canada:
http://www.gg.ca/

Prime Minister of Canada:
http://pm.gc.ca/

Canadian Charter of Rights and Freedoms:
http://canada.gc.ca/Loireg/charte/const_en.html

British Columbia Legislative Assembly:
http://www.legis.gov.bc.ca/

Alberta Legislative Assembly:
http://www.assembly.ab.ca/

Saskatchewan Legislative Assembly:
http://www.legassembly.sk.ca

Manitoba Legislative Assembly:
http://www.gov.mb.ca/leg-asmb/index.html

Ontario Legislative Assembly:
http://www.ontla.on.ca

National Assembly of Quebec:
http://www.assnat.qc.ca

New Brunswick Legislative Assembly:
http://www.gov.nb.ca/legis/index.htm

Nova Scotia Legislative Assembly:
http://www.gov.ns.ca/legi/index.htm

Prince Edward Island Legislative Assembly:
http://www.gov.pe.ca/leg/index.asp

Newfoundland Legislative Assembly:
http://public.gov.nf.ca/house/

Yukon Territory Assembly:
http://www.gov.yk.ca/legassem.html

Northwest Territories Assembly:
http://www.assembly.gov.nt.ca/LEG/mindexorg.html

Territory of Nunavut:
http://www.icon.gov.nu.ca/english/aboutOIC.html

Inuktitut alphabet font download:
http://www.nunavut.com/technology/english/download.html

PARLIAMENT OF AUSTRALIA

If you want basic information about the Australian political system, your Destination No. 1 is Bryan Palmer's Australian Politics. Bryan's site is one of the most excellent politicial Web sites I have ever seen. It's superbly laid out, loads like a dream, and has an easy to navigate frameset design.

Bryan has a superb explanation of Responsible Government and an excellently detailed short history of Australia's greatest constitutional crisis, the Gough Whitlam Dismissal affair of 1975. I remember following that story very closely, even though I was only 15 years old at the time. My opinion: the Dismissal Crisis occurred because Australia has a co-equal Senate which was able to deny "supply" to Whitlam's Government. It was my memory of this event in particular that led me to propose a College of Legates without legislative authority.

The Web site of the Australian Parliament is functional, but not as spectacularly excellent as the Canadian Parliament site. The site has an overview page, the Prime Minister's page, the text of the Australian constitution, and pages for the Senate and the House of Representatives—the two co-equal chambers of the Parliament (which is a large weakness of the Australian system). Australia's Head of State is the Governor General; the current holder of the office is Sir William Deane.

You can also find out about the States of Australia and their Parliaments: Western Australia, South Australia, Victoria, New South Wales, Queensland, and Tasmania, and the Australian Capital Territory and the Northern Territory.

Bryan Palmer's Australian Politics:
http://members.dingoblue.net.au/~bdpalmer

Palmer's explanation of Responsible Government:
http://members.dingoblue.net.au/~bdpalmer/conventions/rg.htm

Appendix IV

Palmer's history of the Gough Whitlam Dismissal Crisis of 1975:
http://members.dingoblue.net.au/~bdpalmer/conventions/
dismissal.htm

Parliament of Australia:
http://www.aph.gov.au/

Australian Parliament overview page:
http://www.aph.gov.au/parl.htm

Prime Minister of Australia:
http://www.pm.gov.au/

Australian Constitution:
http://www.aph.gov.au/senate/general/constitution/index.htm

Australian Senate:
http://www.aph.gov.au/senate/index.htm

Australian House of Representatives:
http://www.aph.gov.au/house/index.htm

Governor General of Australia:
http://www.aph.gov.au/library/gov/ggrole.htm

Sir William Deane, current Governor General of Australia:
http://www.aph.gov.au/library/gov/govgbiog.htm

Western Australia Parliament:
http://www.parliament.wa.gov.au/

South Australia Parliament:
http://www.pics.sa.gov.au/

Victoria Parliament
http://www.parliament.vic.gov.au/

New South Wales Parliament:
http://www.parliament.nsw.gov.au/

Queensland Parliament:
http://www.parliament.qld.gov.au/

Tasmania Parliament:
http://www.parliament.tas.gov.au/

Australian Capital Territory Parliament:
http://www.legassembly.act.gov.au/

Northern Territory Parliament:
http://www.nt.gov.au/lant/

PARLIAMENT OF NEW ZEALAND

There are two main New Zealand Parliament sites; one has a straightforward governmental focus, while the other is mainly designed for schools. Both are excellently done, much better than the Australian site.

There is also a list of current New Zealand Members of Parliament; the number increased to 120 in 1996 when New Zealand rashly adopted a partial proportional representation system, ignoring the disasters of proportional representation in Israel, Italy, Germany, and other places. The schools site has a first-class image map of the Parliament buildings in downtown Wellington, the capital.

My first experience with leadership under a parliamentary government was my year in New Zealand 1976–1977, when Robert Muldoon (1921–1992) was Prime Minister of New Zealand.

An excellent New Zealand Government gateway site provides links to everything public-sector in the Land of the Long White Cloud.

The New Zealand Government has apparently contracted out some of its on-line law storage to an outfit called The Knowledge Basket, which has a complete listing of the many and various laws of

New Zealand. One key statute, which I consulted when I "quilted" the CRG draft constitution, was the Constitution Act of 1986, which despite its name is a mere repealable law and not a *lex supremis.*

There are also some good politics links at the Web site of the University of Canterbury at Christchurch.

Parliament of New Zealand (political focus):
http://www.parliament.govt.nz/

Parliament of New Zealand (education focus):
http://www.ps.parliament.govt.nz/

List of New Zealand MPs:
http://www.parliament.govt.nz/mps.htm

Sir Robert Muldoon (1921–1992):
http://www.wijinmusic.com/blackh/sirrob.html

Image-map of New Zealand Parliament buildings in Wellington:
http://www.ps.parliament.govt.nz/building.htm

New Zealand Government gateway site:
http://www.govt.nz/

"The Knowledge Basket":
http://www.knowledge-basket.co.nz/welcome.html

Knowledge Basket's listing of New Zealand laws:
http://www.knowledge-basket.co.nz/gpprint/gpprint/acts/actlists.html

New Zealand Constitution Act 1986:
http://www.knowledge-basket.co.nz/gpprint/acts/public/text/1986/an/114.html

Politics links at the University of Canterbury, Christchurch:
http://www.pols.canterbury.ac.nz/links.htm

PARLIAMENT OF IRELAND/OIREACHTAS na hÉIREANN

Many of the provisions of the Constitution of the Irish Republic were important in composing the New Form draft. This Constitution was drafted in 1937 under the leadership of legendary Irish leader Eamonn deValera.

The Irish Constitution is the only one in English that spells out certain provisions, like the appointment of a Cabinet and a Prime Minister; amazingly, the British-derived constitutions leave that to custom! Surprisingly, the Irish Government Web site doesn't have a copy of its own constitution on it, but borrows it from the Maths Department of historic Trinity College Dublin.

Learning about Irish government requires learning a few words in Irish, such as Uachtarain (President); Oireachtas (Parliament); Seanad (Senate); Dáil Éireann (House of Deputies); and Taoiseach (Prime Minister). You can also read a Welcome (Fáilte) in Irish from the President of Ireland, Mrs. Mary Leneghan McAleese. Not surprisingly, many pages on the Irish Government site have links to versions in Irish.

Two of the leading political parties in Ireland are Fianna Fail ("Soldiers of Destiny") and Fine Gael ("Family of the Irish"). Links to other parties are found on the Irish Government pages. If you search through the party sites, and examine some of the election results (such as Taoiseach Bertie Ahern's Dublin Central constituency) you will see why I thought the "single transferable vote" and multi-member constituencies were better left behind.

Constitution of the Irish Republic:
http://www.maths.tcd.ie/pub/Constitution/index.html

Biography of Eamonn deValera:
http://www.irlgov.ie/aras/devalera.htm

Irish Government Web site:
http://www.irlgov.ie/frmain.htm

Trinity College, Dublin:
http://www.tcd.ie

President of Ireland (Uachtarain na hÉireann):
http://www.irlgov.ie/aras/

Parliament of Ireland (Oireachtas na hÉrieann):
http://www.irlgov.ie/oireachtas

Senate of Ireland (Seanad Érieann):
http://www.irlgov.ie/oireachtas/senator.html

House of Deputies (Dáil Éireann)
http://www.irlgov.ie/oireachtas/deputy.html

Prime Minister of Ireland (Taoiseach na hÉireann):
http://www.irlgov.ie/taoiseach/welcome/default.htm

Greeting from the President of Ireland (in Irish):
http://www.irlgov.ie/aras/failte.htm

Biography of the President, Mrs. McAleese:
http://www.irlgov.ie/aras/welcome.htm

Fianna Fail political party:
http://www.fiannafail.ie

Fine Gael political party:
http://www.finegael.com

Links to other Irish political parties:
http://www.irlgov.ie/oireachtas/parties.html

Election results, Dublin Central constituency, 1997 general election:
http://www.fiannafail.ie/constituencies/ge1997/11count.htm

PARLIAMENT OF INDIA

India, the world's largest democracy, has managed, stumblingly, to hold on the Westminster form of government that it inherited from the British. In spring 1999, the Bharatia Janata Party (BJP) government fell—by a single vote. In September, however, the BJP and its allies returned to power with a comfortable majority. Tensions with next-door Pakistan are hot once again over the Kashmir question. The two countries have gone to war four times since independence in 1947, and now, both of them have nukes.

An excellent site on this election, with constituency-level details, is the IndiaMap: Elections 1999, which claims to present "a dynamic ringside account & analysis of the elections to Parliament in the world's largest democracy."

There is an Official Parliament of India site with links to all the important parts of the Centre (as Indians refer to their national government). The lower, responsible house of Parliament is the Lok Sabha. The Government is governed by the Constitution of India, a document which could use some substantital weight reduction. Some useful, and mercifully short, summaries of Indian politics are found on the IndiaMart business-focused Web site.

IndiaMap: Elections 1999:
http://www.indiamap.com/elections

Parliament of India Web site:
http://alfa.nic.in/welcome2.htm

Lok Sabha (lower house of Parliament):
http://alfa.nic.in/lsbak.htm

Constitution of India:
http://164.100.24.8/const/a1.html

IndiaMart political summaries:
http://www.indiamart.com/finance/government_india/parliament_india.html

OTHER RESOURCES

Westminster-style Governments aren't just found in large countries; smaller ones have them too. The Parliament of Trinidad and Tobago is one example. You can also expand your constitutional horizons by examining the constitutions of The Republic of China (Taiwan), Germany, and Japan. All of these sites are in English.

The law school of the University of Richmond has a link to darn near every constitution in the world most in English, many in their country's language(s).

You should examine the Web site of Berlin-based Transparency International and to their Corruption Perceptions Index. Find out why the U.S. is ranked, along with Austria, as only the 17th least corrupt country in the world. It will make you think.

Trinidad and Tobago Parliament:
http://www.ttparliament.org

Republic of China constitution (in English):
http://www.oop.gov.tw/roc/charter/echarter.htm

Federal Republic of Germany constitution (in English):
http://www.jura.uni-sb.de/law/GG/gg0.html

Japanese constitution (in English):
http://www.ntt.co.jp/japan/constitution/english-Constitution.html

Links to other constitutions, from the University of Richmond law school:
http://www.urich.edu/jpjones/confinder/const.htm

Transparency International:
http://www.transparency.de/

Transparency International Corruption Perceptions Indez:
http://www.transparency.de/documents/cpi/index.html